UFO Catcher Ken™

presents

There is No Shrimp ...
And Other Lies My Mother Told Me

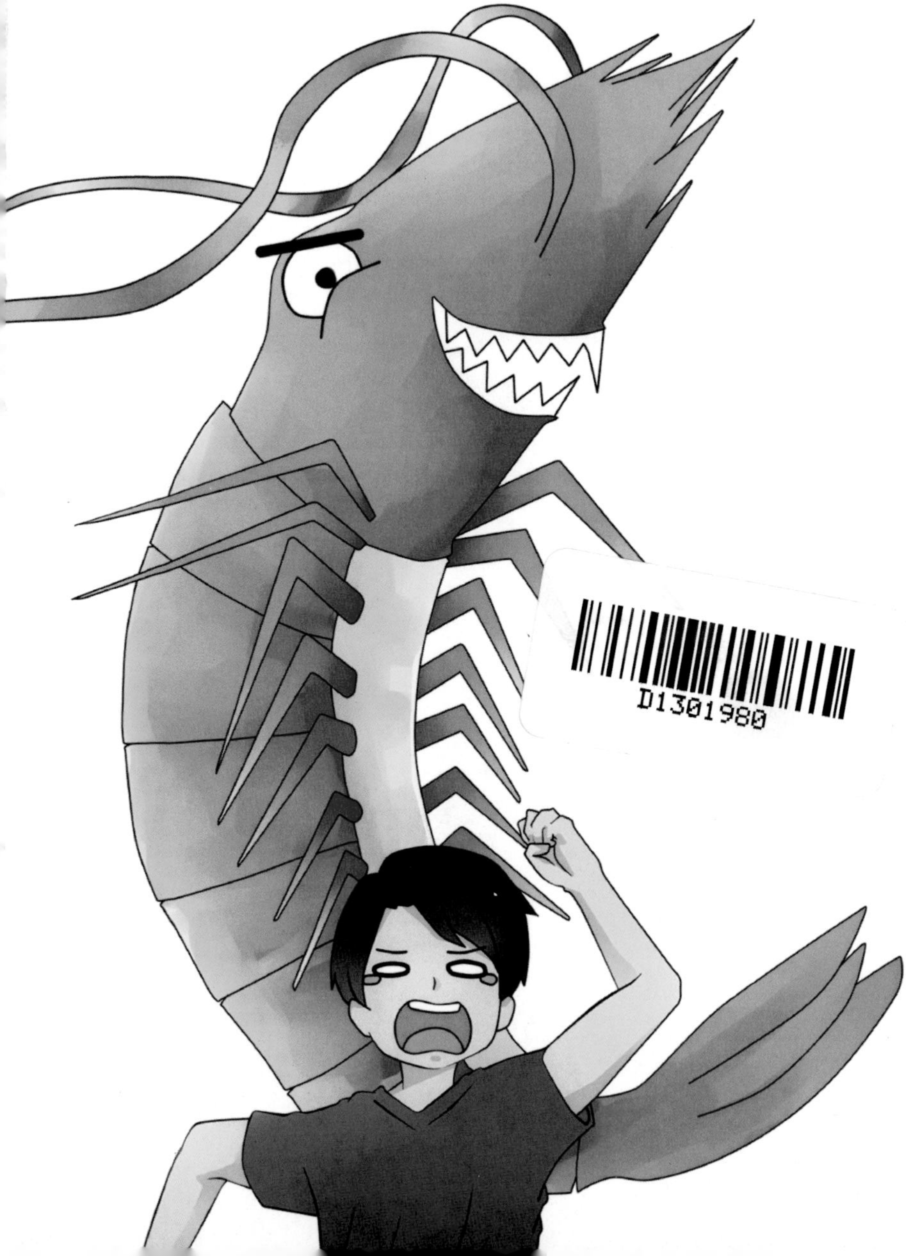

UFO Catcher Ken Presents: There is No Shrimp … And Other Lies My Mother Told Me

Story and characters by Kenny Loui
Art by Yamawe

Published by UFO Comics
Editor: Kenny Loui

Printed in the United States
First Printing: July 2023

The stories herein are based on actual events and personal experiences of the author. Names, appearances, and other identifying details of individuals and places have been changed to protect the privacy of the innocent and not-so-innocent... because the author a nice guy that way. Details of certain events have also been modified for the reasons mentioned above. Thus, any resemblance to actual persons, living or dead (or ascended... a Stargate reference for any SG-1 fans out there)--with the exception of the author, his parents, and his favorite kindergarten teacher--is purely coincidental.

Did you really read this copyright page in its entirety, from beginning to end? If so, you're awesome! Enjoy, 楽しんで！

ISBN: 979-8-9867300-3-5 (paperback)
ISBN: 979-8-9867300-4-2 (e-book)

Dedicated to my mother, who always told me sweet, little lies.

Mom...
Before the
world "evolved"
into color. ᵔ◡ᵔ

Also dedicated to Mrs. O'Brien, who always set the record straight.

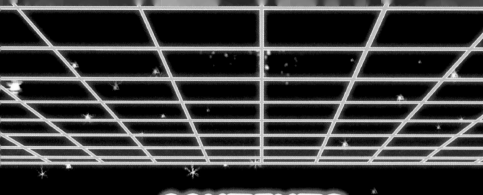

CONTENTS

UFO Catcher Ken™

presents

There is No Shrimp ... And Other Lies My Mother Told Me

Story by
KENNY LOUI

Art by
YAMAWE

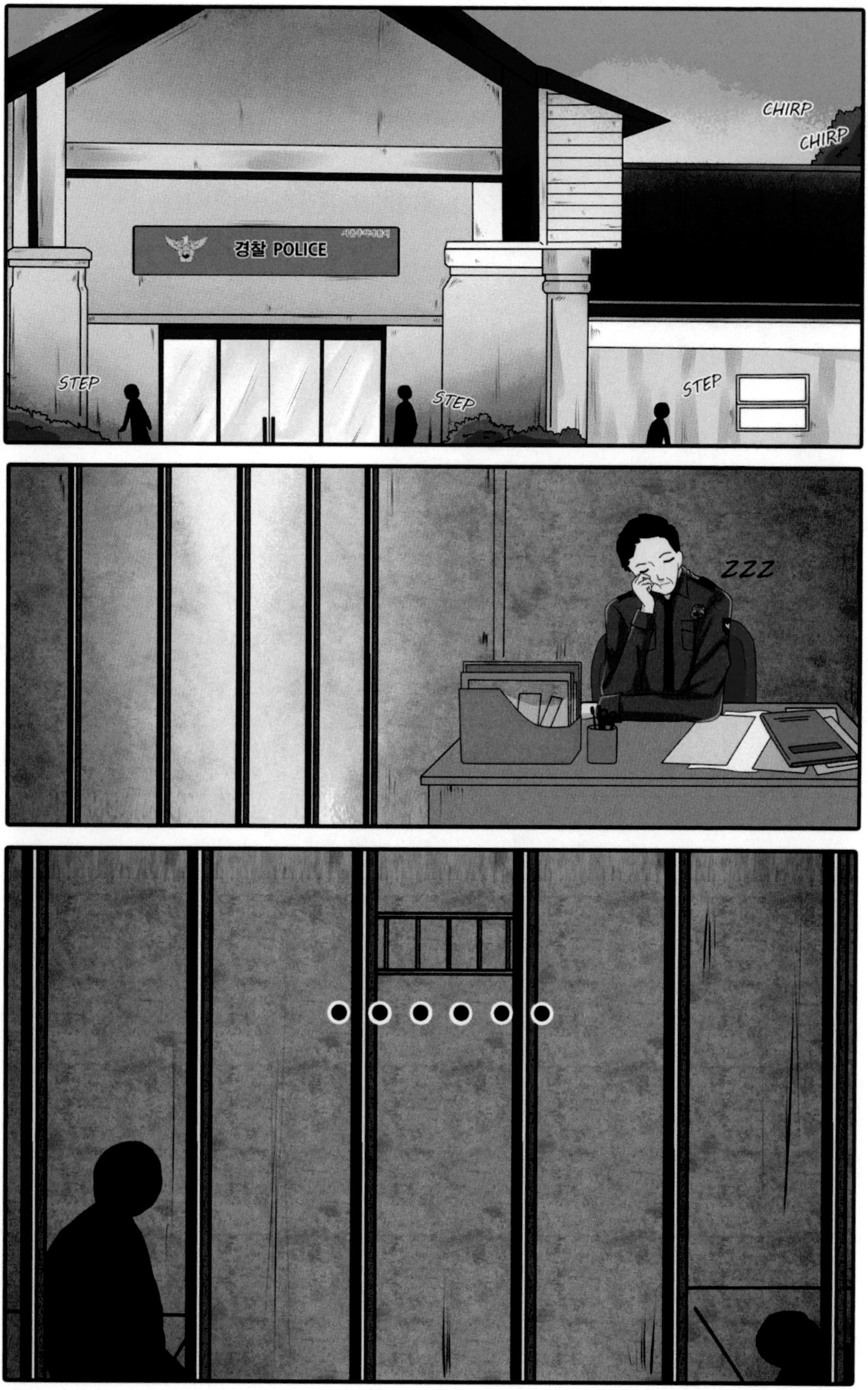
경찰 POLICE
CHIRP
CHIRP
STEP
STEP
STEP
ZZZ
......

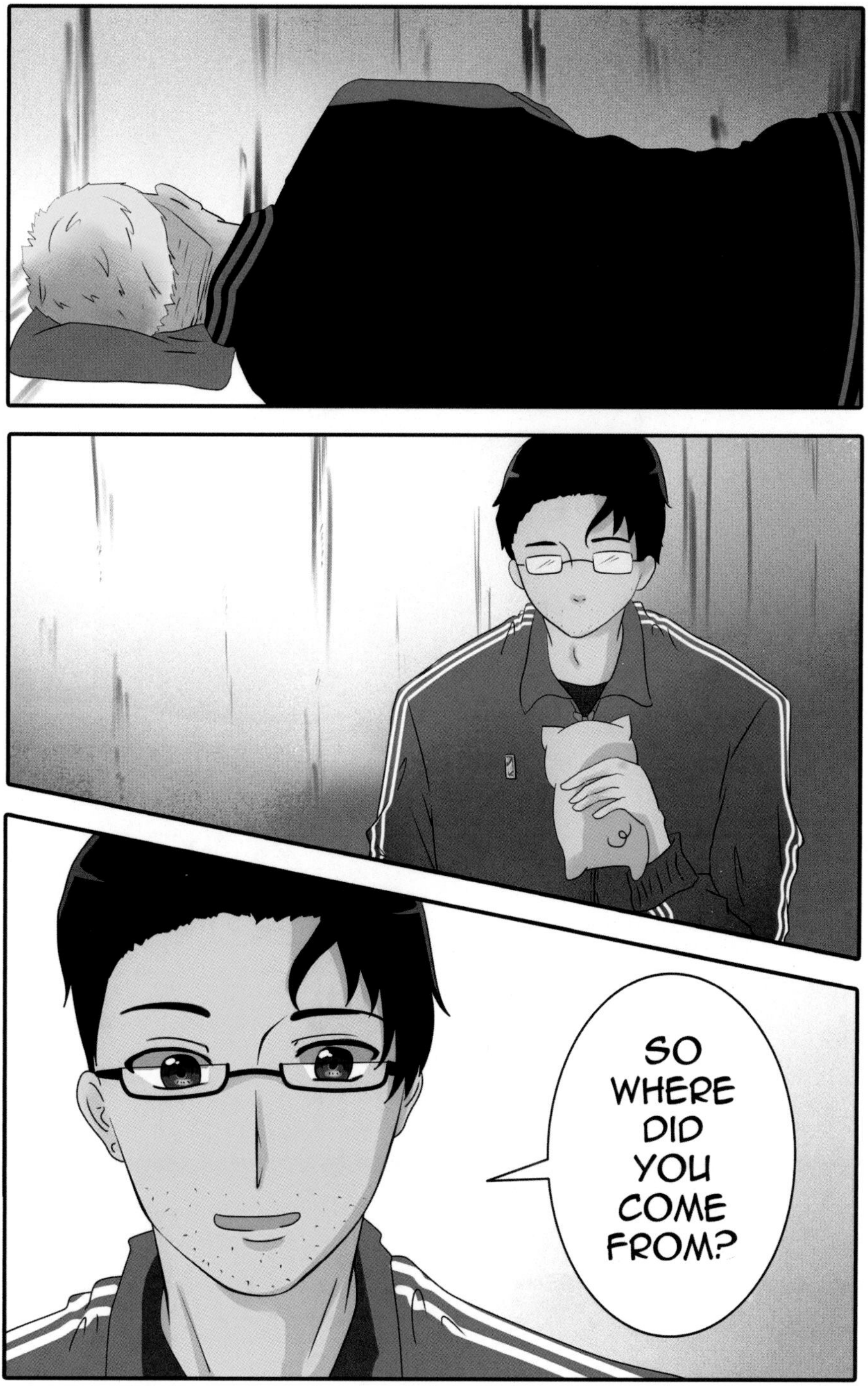
SO WHERE DID YOU COME FROM?

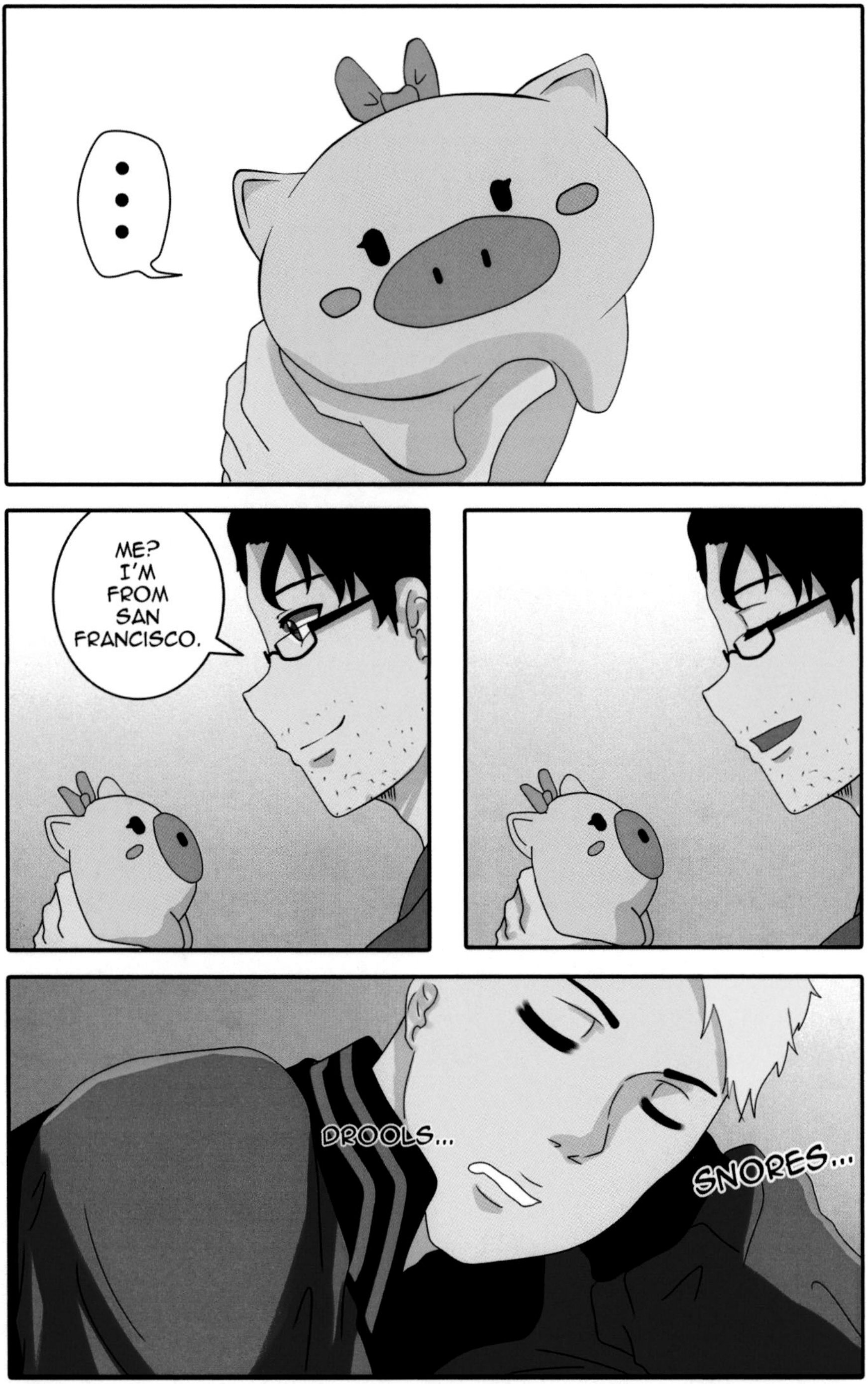
...
ME? I'M FROM SAN FRANCISCO.
DROOLS...
SNORES...

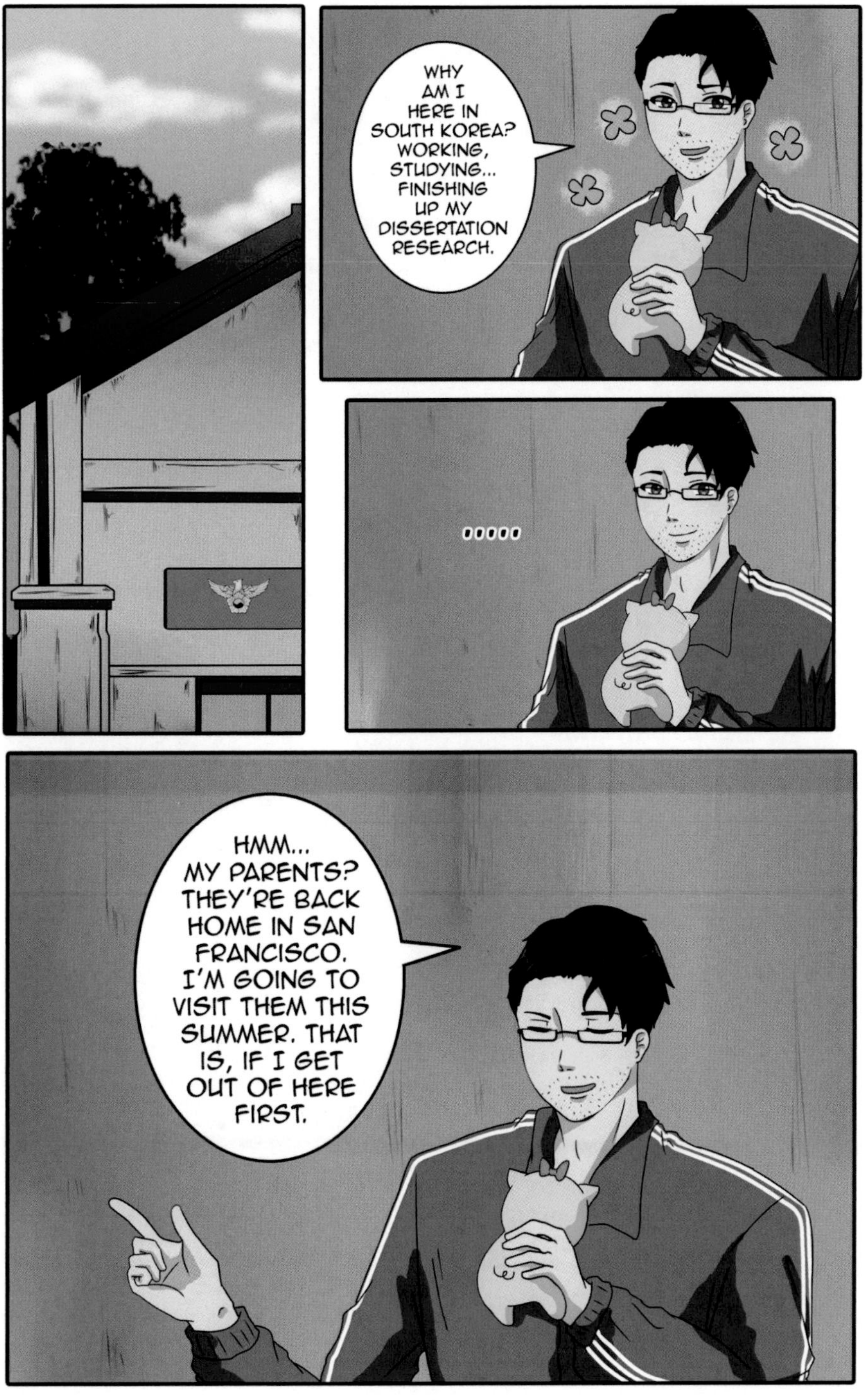
WHY AM I HERE IN SOUTH KOREA? WORKING, STUDYING... FINISHING UP MY DISSERTATION RESEARCH.
.....
HMM... MY PARENTS? THEY'RE BACK HOME IN SAN FRANCISCO. I'M GOING TO VISIT THEM THIS SUMMER. THAT IS, IF I GET OUT OF HERE FIRST.

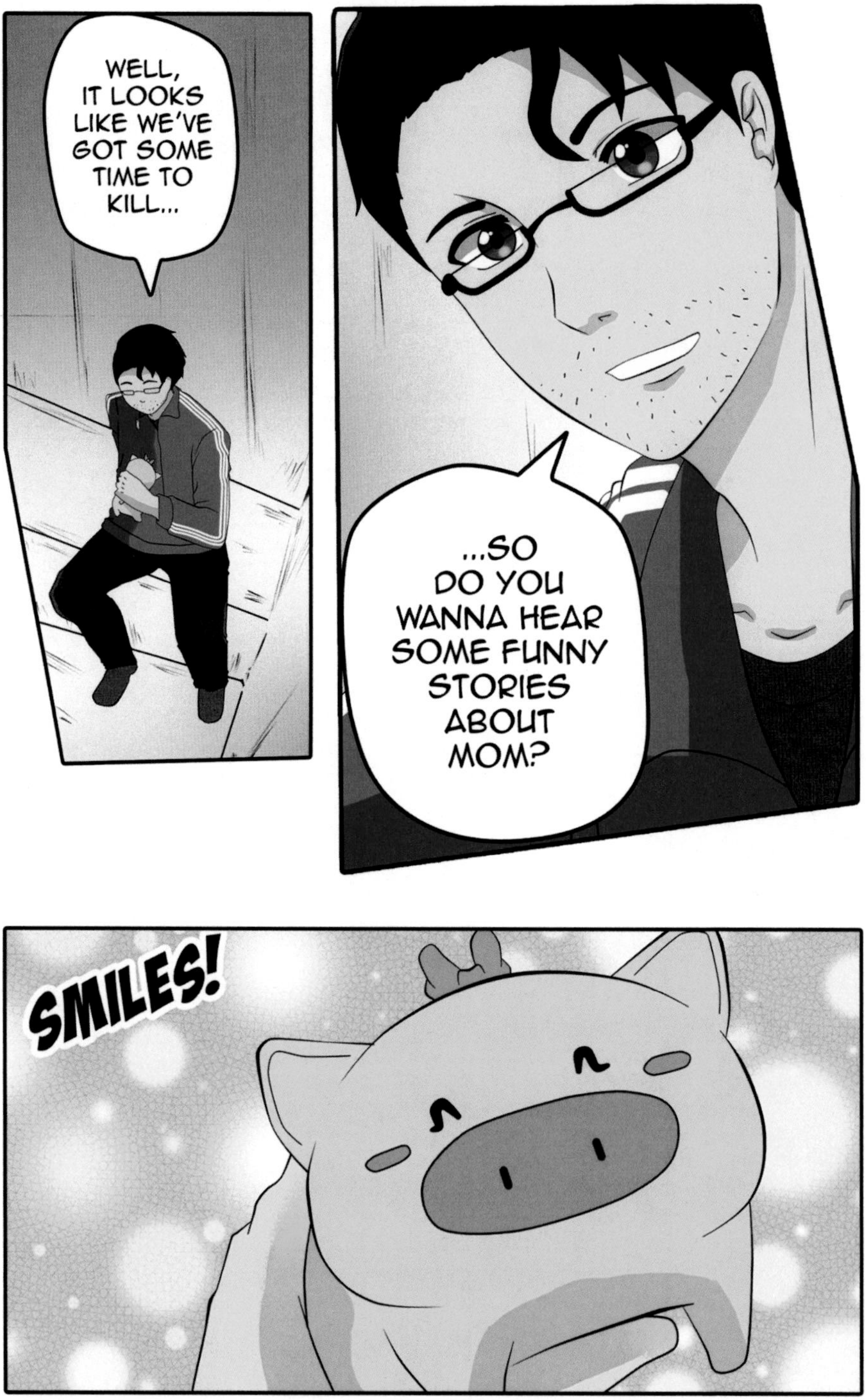
WELL, IT LOOKS LIKE WE'VE GOT SOME TIME TO KILL...
...SO DO YOU WANNA HEAR SOME FUNNY STORIES ABOUT MOM?
SMILES!

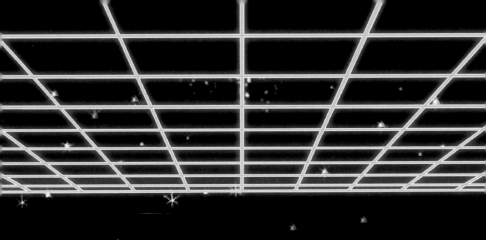

The Evolution of Color

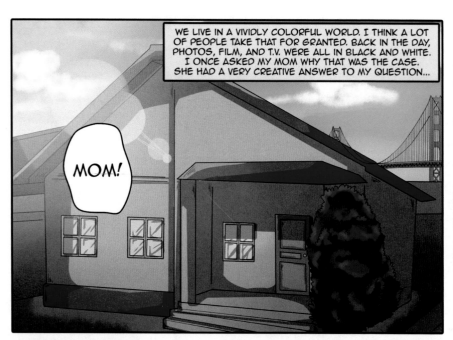

WE LIVE IN A VIVIDLY COLORFUL WORLD. I THINK A LOT OF PEOPLE TAKE THAT FOR GRANTED. BACK IN THE DAY, PHOTOS, FILM, AND T.V. WERE ALL IN BLACK AND WHITE. I ONCE ASKED MY MOM WHY THAT WAS THE CASE. SHE HAD A VERY CREATIVE ANSWER TO MY QUESTION...

MOM!

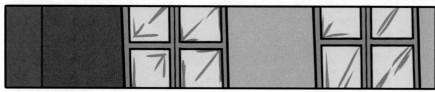

WHY ARE ALL YOUR OLD PHOTOS IN BLACK AND WHITE AND NOT COLOR?

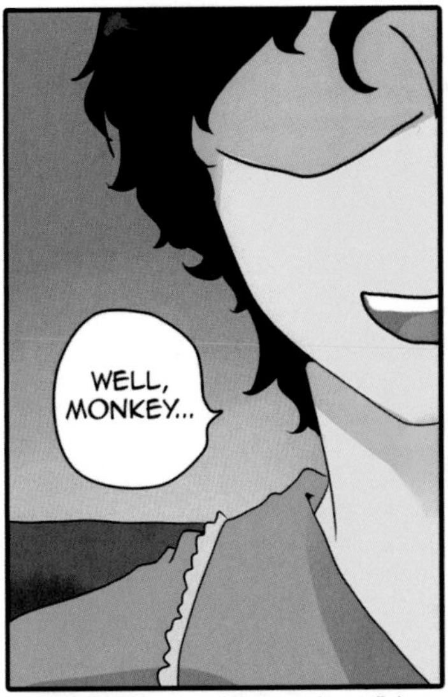
WELL, MONKEY...

*Author's Note:** When I was a kid, my mom always called me "monkey." She said that when I was born, I looked like a "baby monkey," like Goku from *Dragon Ball*.

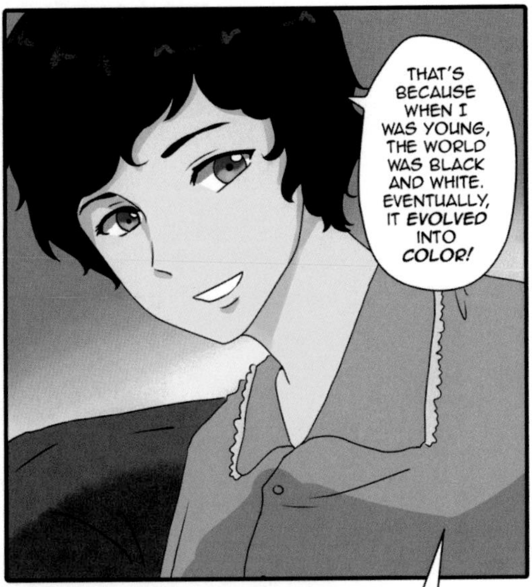
THAT'S BECAUSE WHEN I WAS YOUNG, THE WORLD WAS BLACK AND WHITE. EVENTUALLY, IT EVOLVED INTO COLOR!

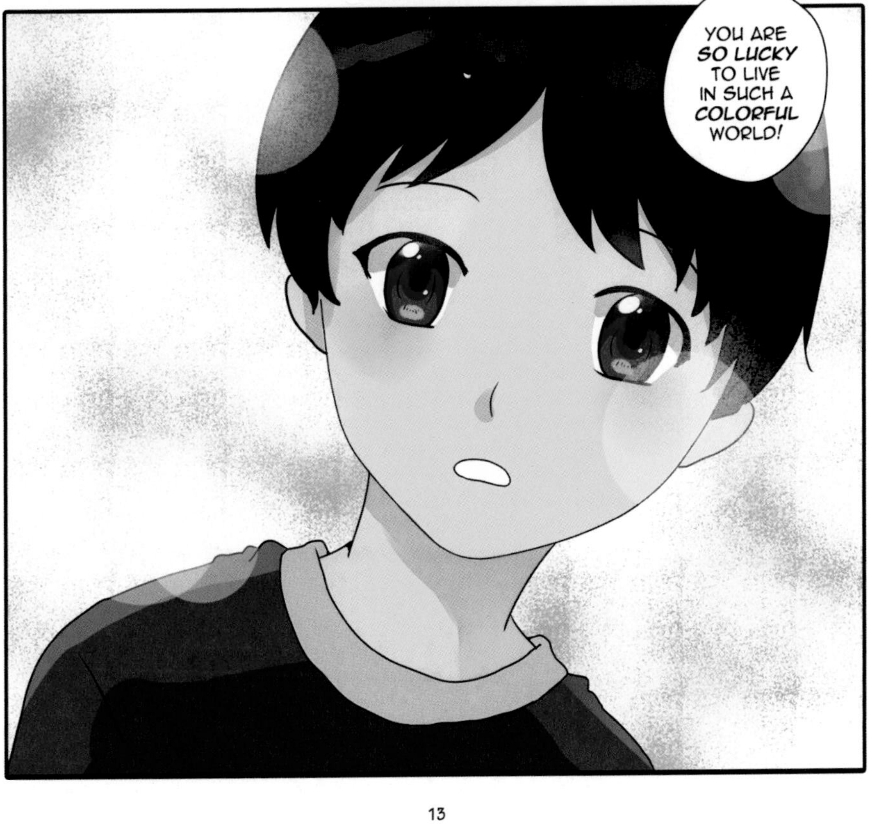
YOU ARE SO LUCKY TO LIVE IN SUCH A COLORFUL WORLD!

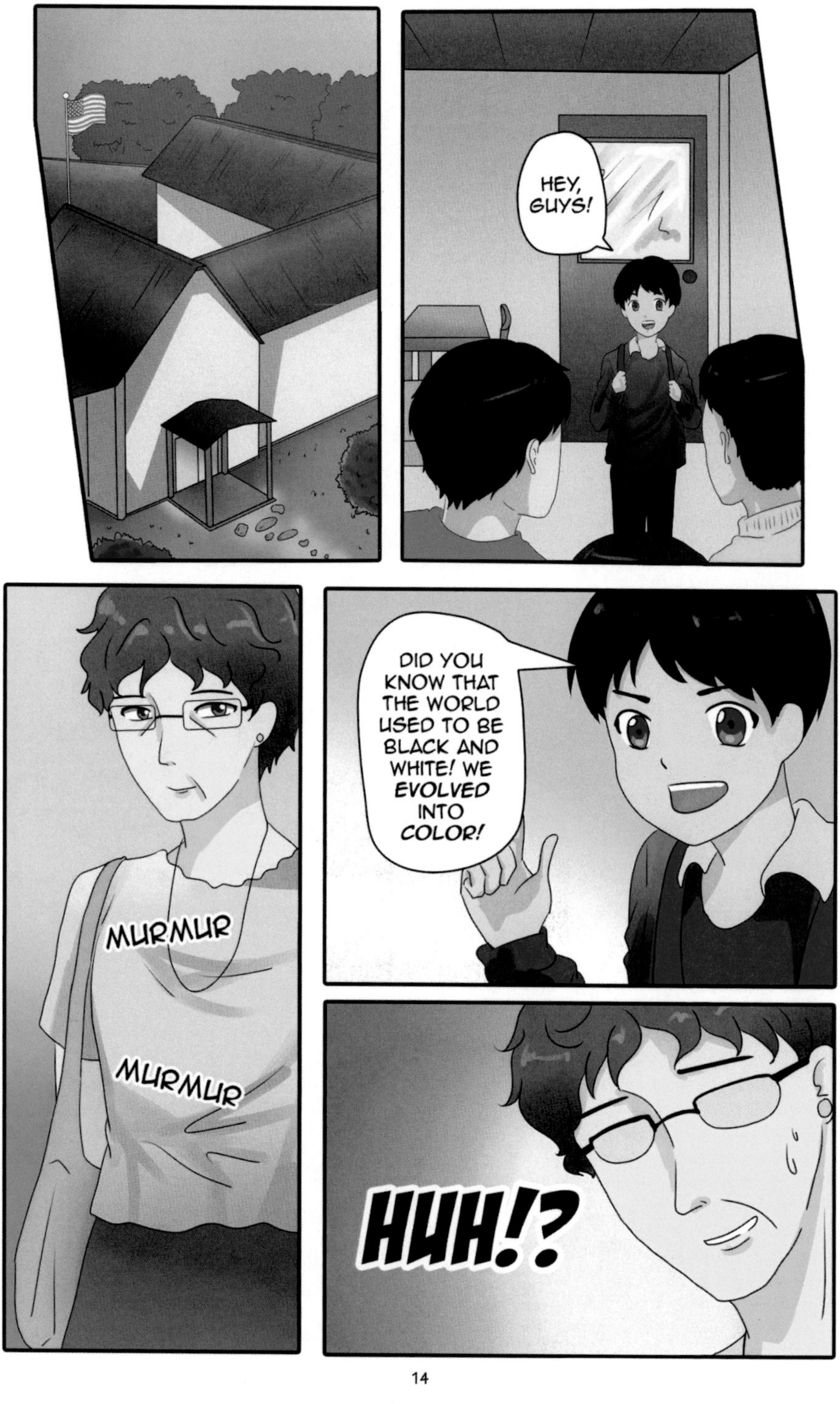
HEY, GUYS!
MURMUR
MURMUR
DID YOU KNOW THAT THE WORLD USED TO BE BLACK AND WHITE! WE EVOLVED INTO COLOR!
HUH!?

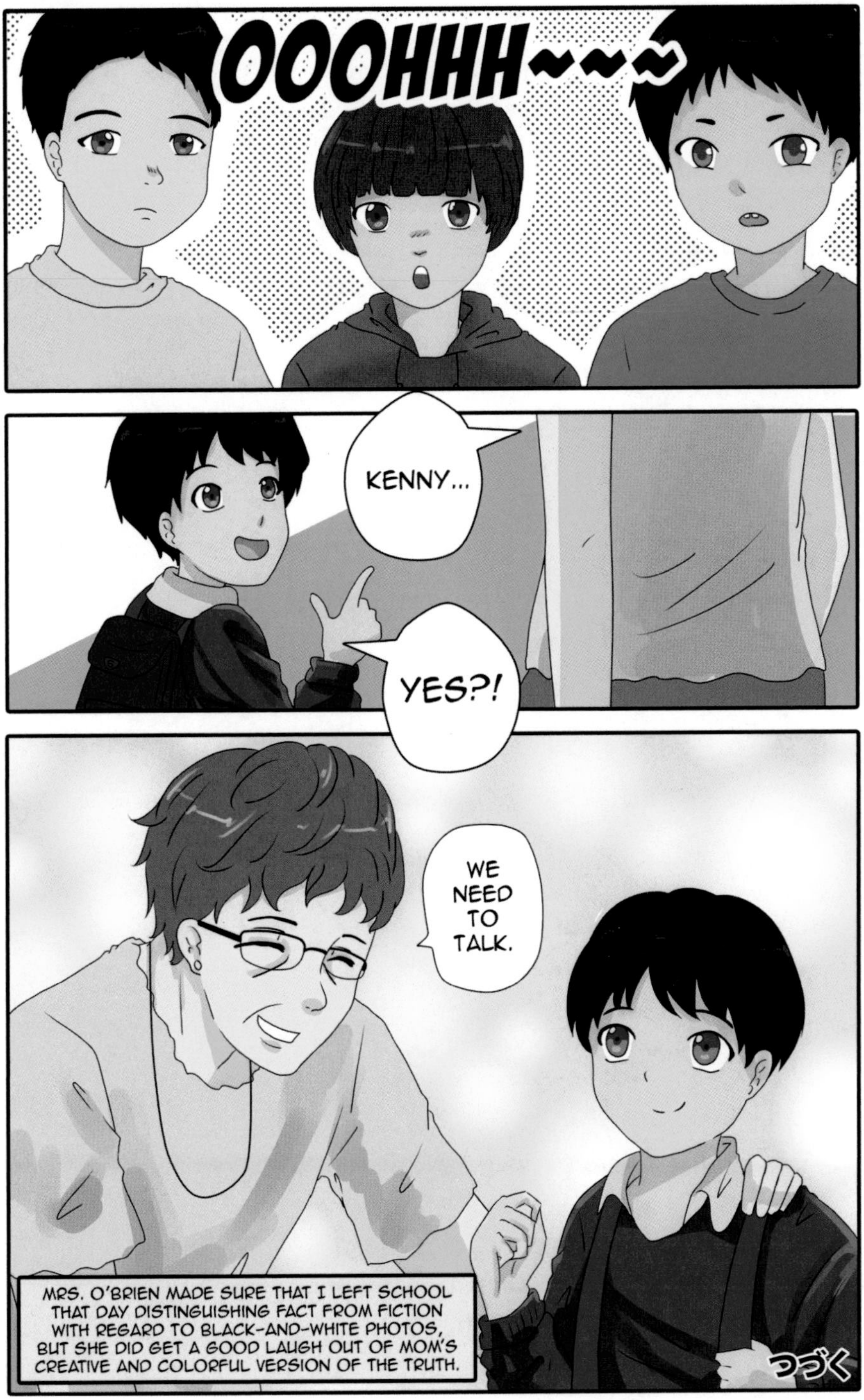
OOOHHH~~~
KENNY...
YES?!
WE NEED TO TALK.
MRS. O'BRIEN MADE SURE THAT I LEFT SCHOOL THAT DAY DISTINGUISHING FACT FROM FICTION WITH REGARD TO BLACK-AND-WHITE PHOTOS, BUT SHE DID GET A GOOD LAUGH OUT OF MOM'S CREATIVE AND COLORFUL VERSION OF THE TRUTH.
つづく

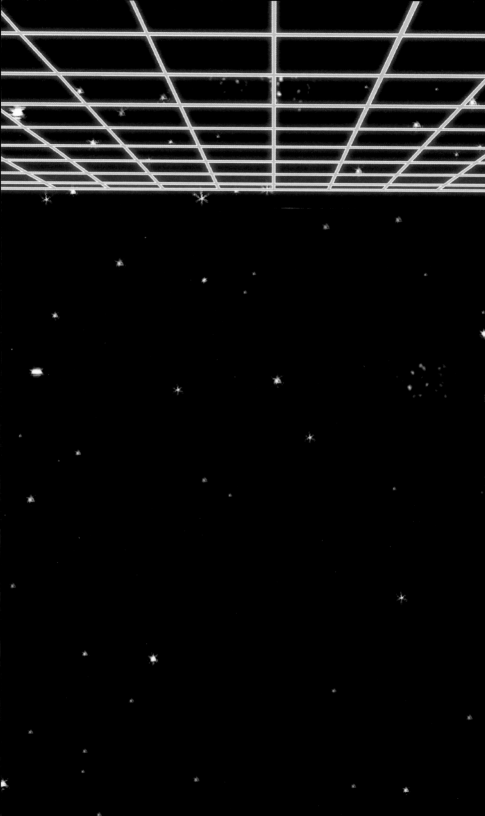

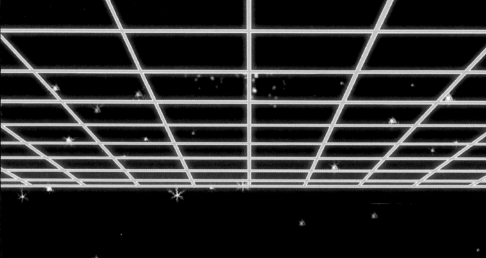

Up, Up, and Away

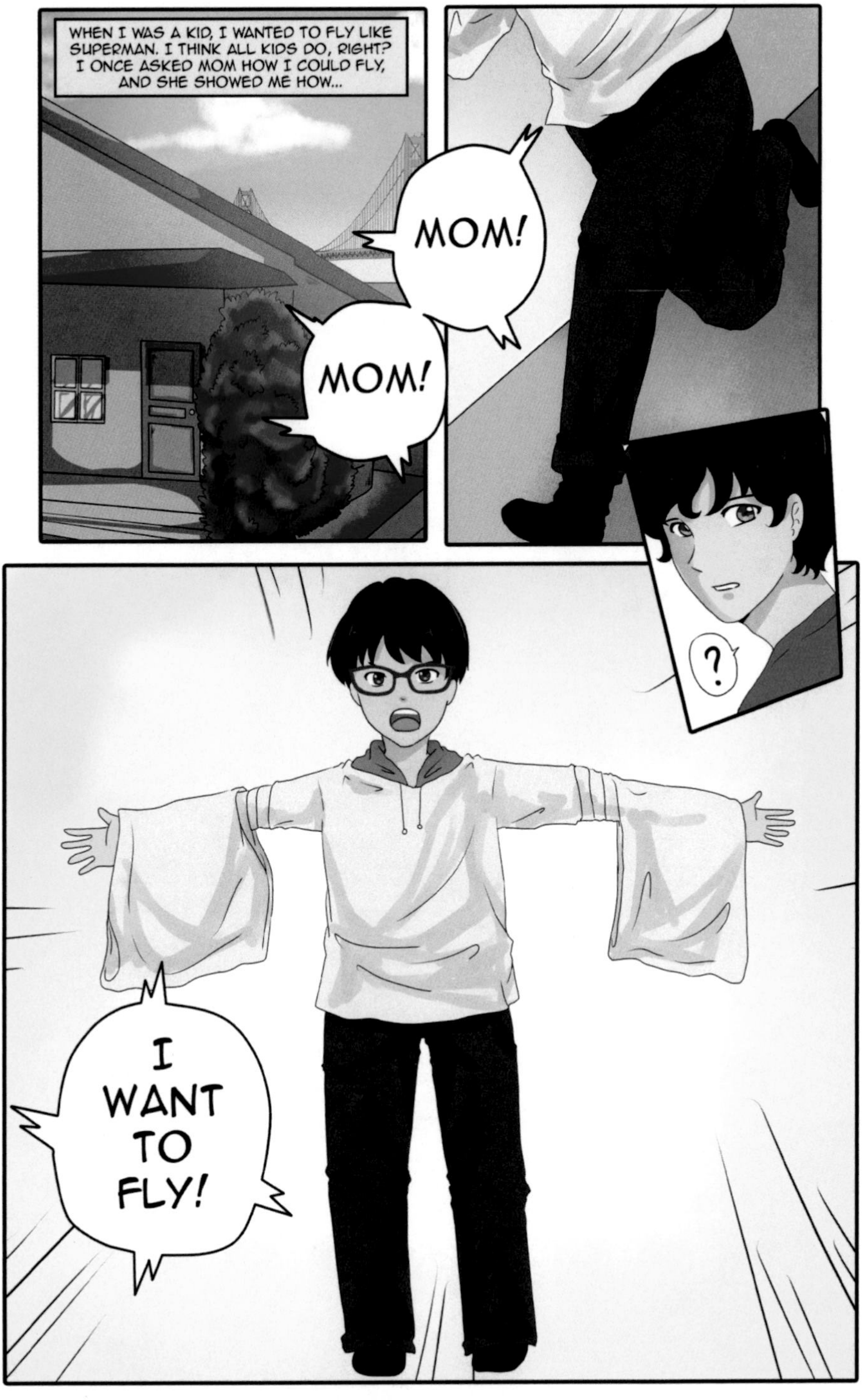
WHEN I WAS A KID, I WANTED TO FLY LIKE SUPERMAN. I THINK ALL KIDS DO, RIGHT? I ONCE ASKED MOM HOW I COULD FLY, AND SHE SHOWED ME HOW...
MOM!
MOM!
?
I WANT TO FLY!

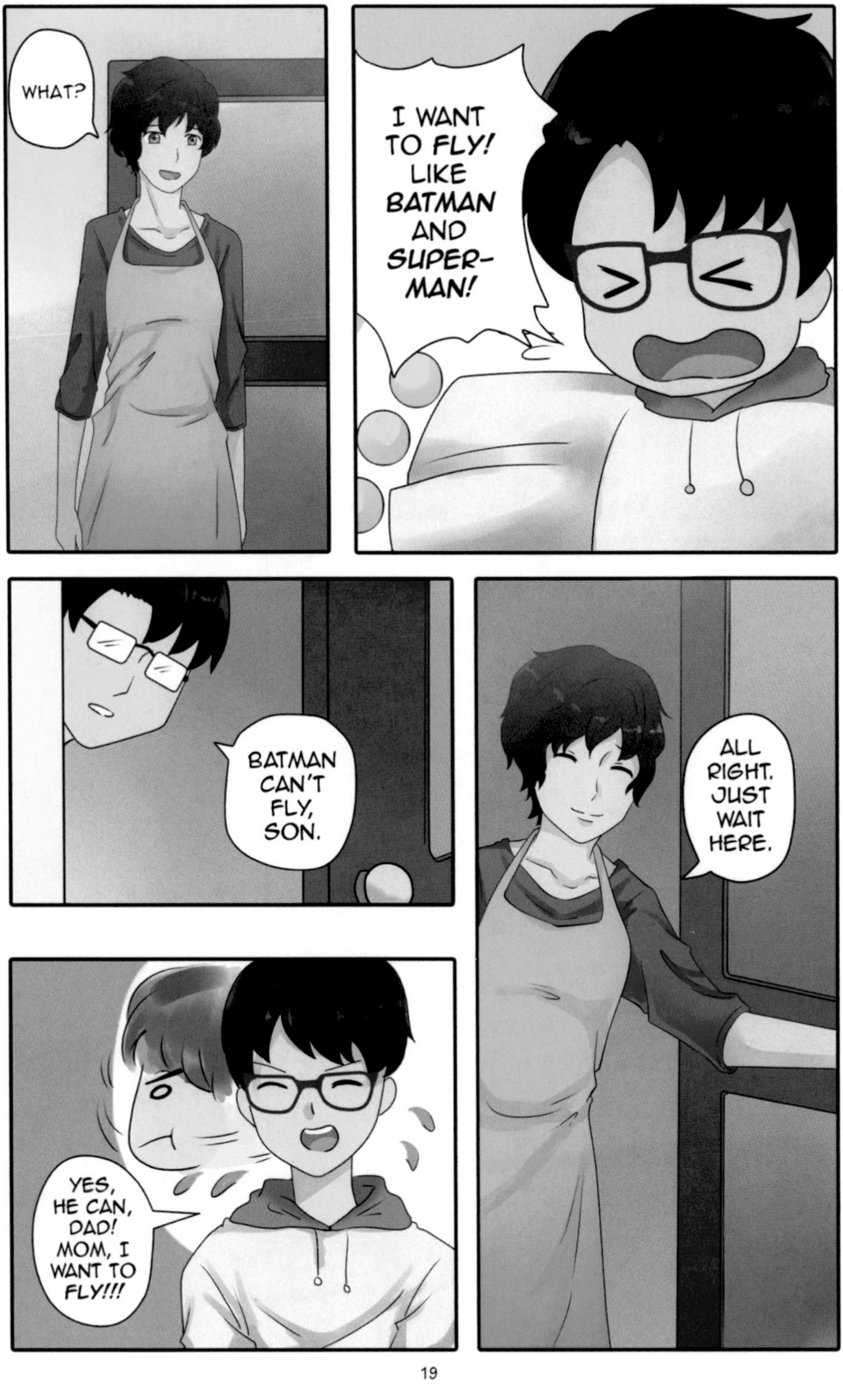
WHAT?
I WANT TO FLY! LIKE BATMAN AND SUPER-MAN!
BATMAN CAN'T FLY, SON.
ALL RIGHT. JUST WAIT HERE.
YES, HE CAN, DAD! MOM, I WANT TO FLY!!!

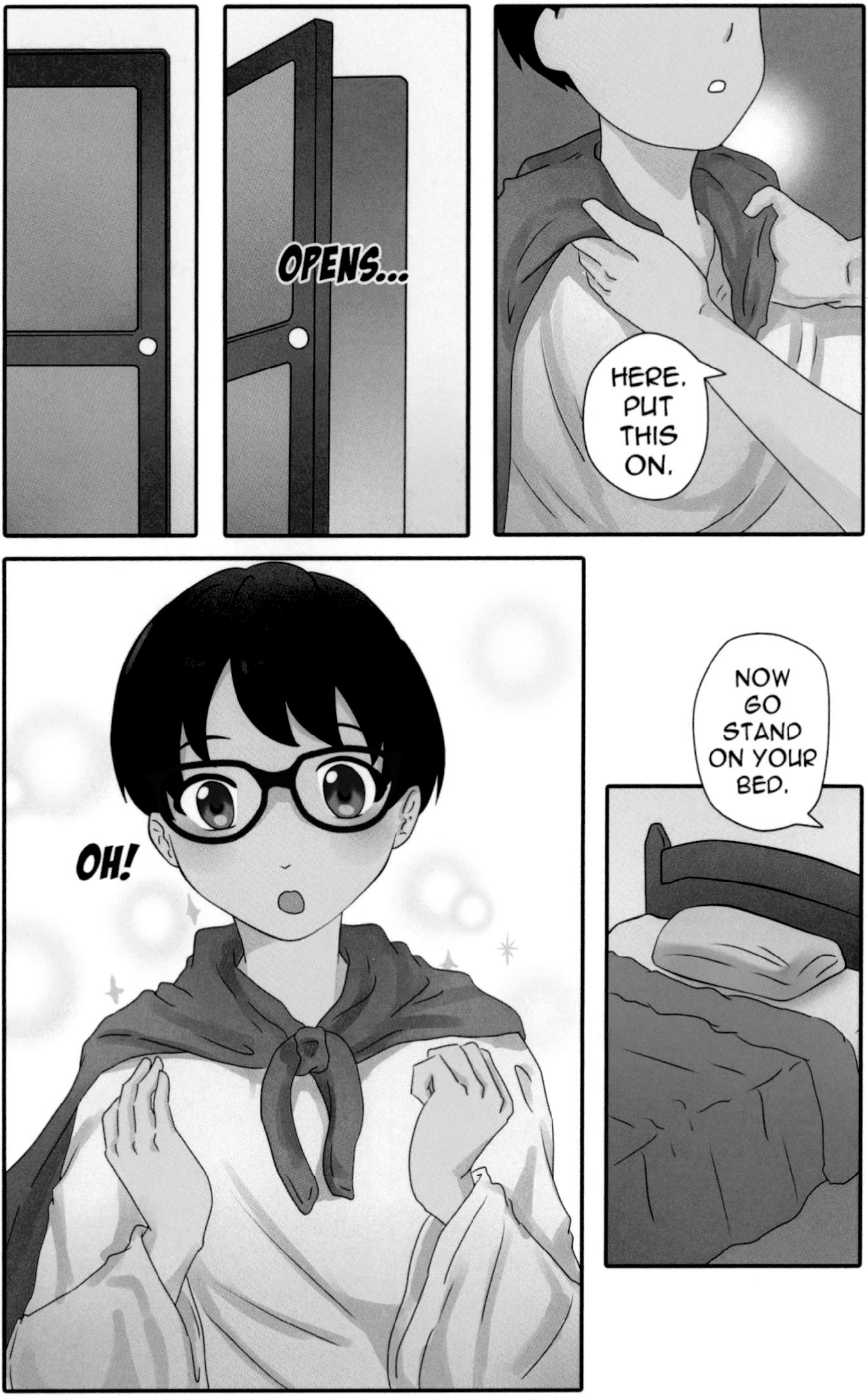
OPENS...
HERE. PUT THIS ON.
OH!
NOW GO STAND ON YOUR BED.

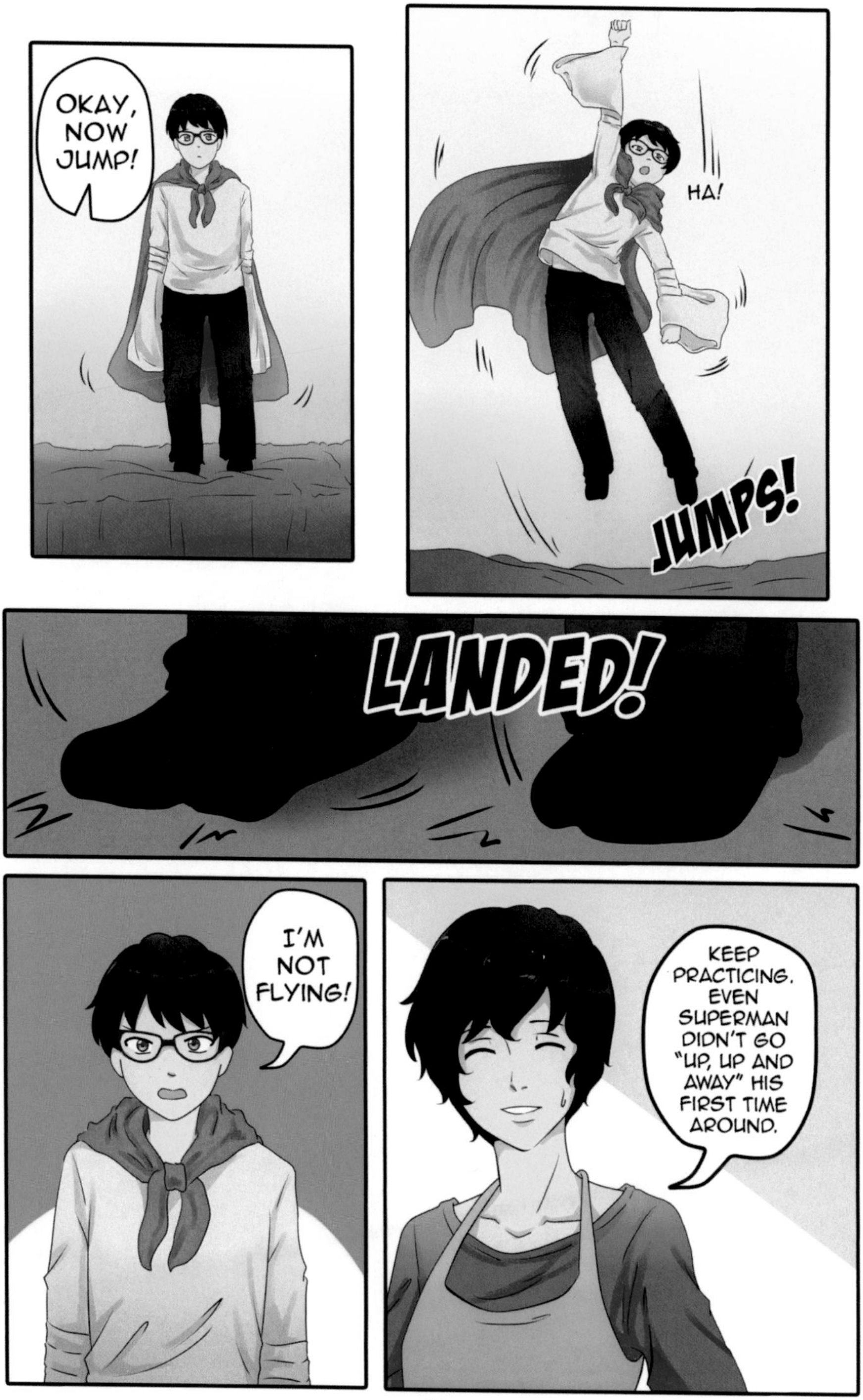
OKAY, NOW JUMP!
HA!
JUMPS!
LANDED!
I'M NOT FLYING!
KEEP PRACTICING. EVEN SUPERMAN DIDN'T GO "UP, UP AND AWAY" HIS FIRST TIME AROUND.

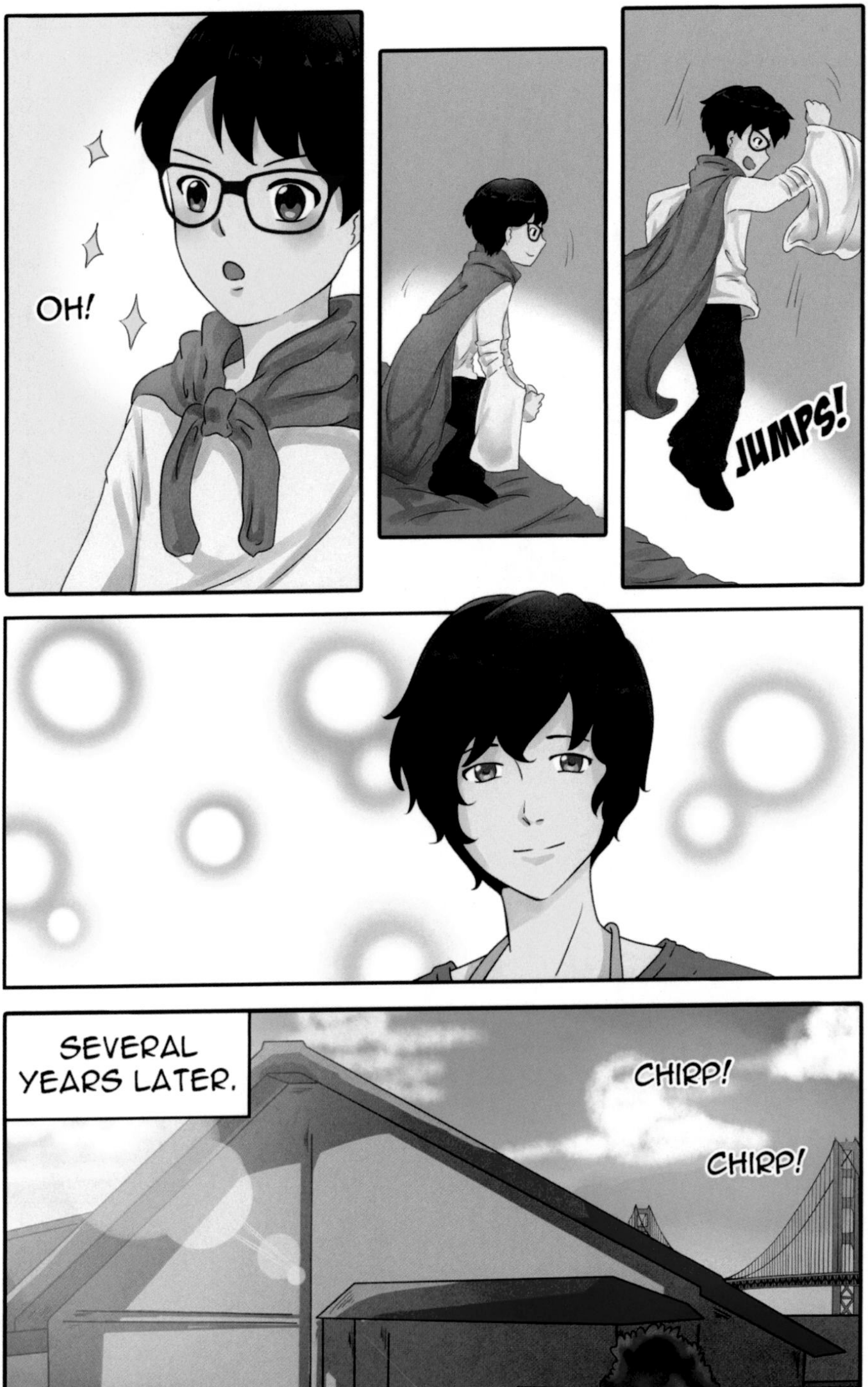
OH!
JUMPS!
SEVERAL YEARS LATER.
CHIRP!
CHIRP!

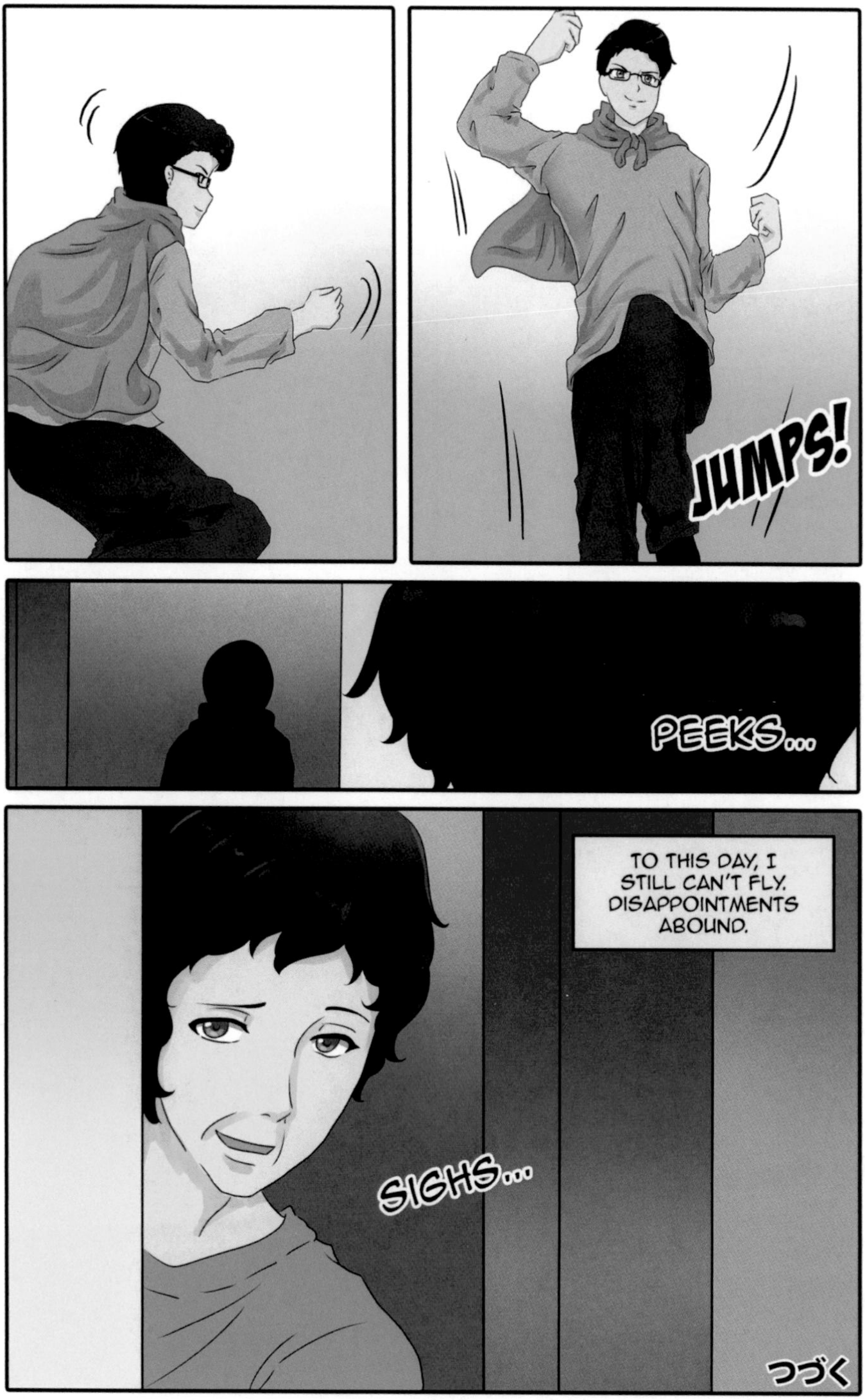
JUMPS!
PEEKS...
TO THIS DAY, I STILL CAN'T FLY. DISAPPOINTMENTS ABOUND.
SIGHS...
つづく

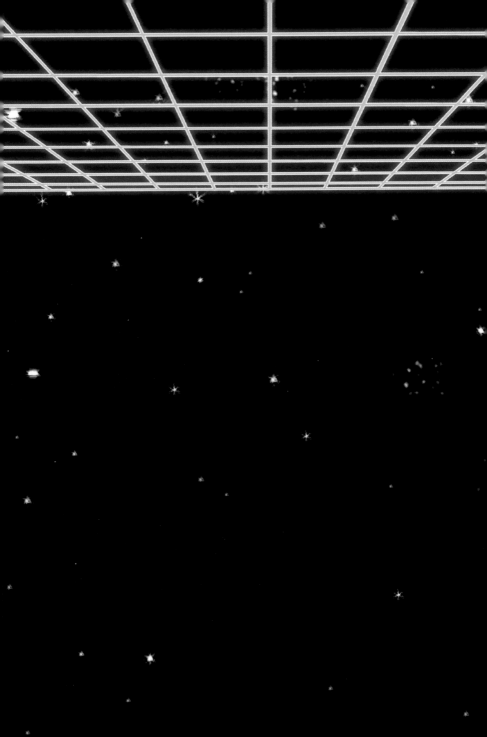

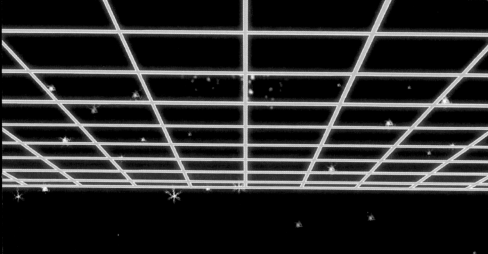

Goodnight, Little T.V. People

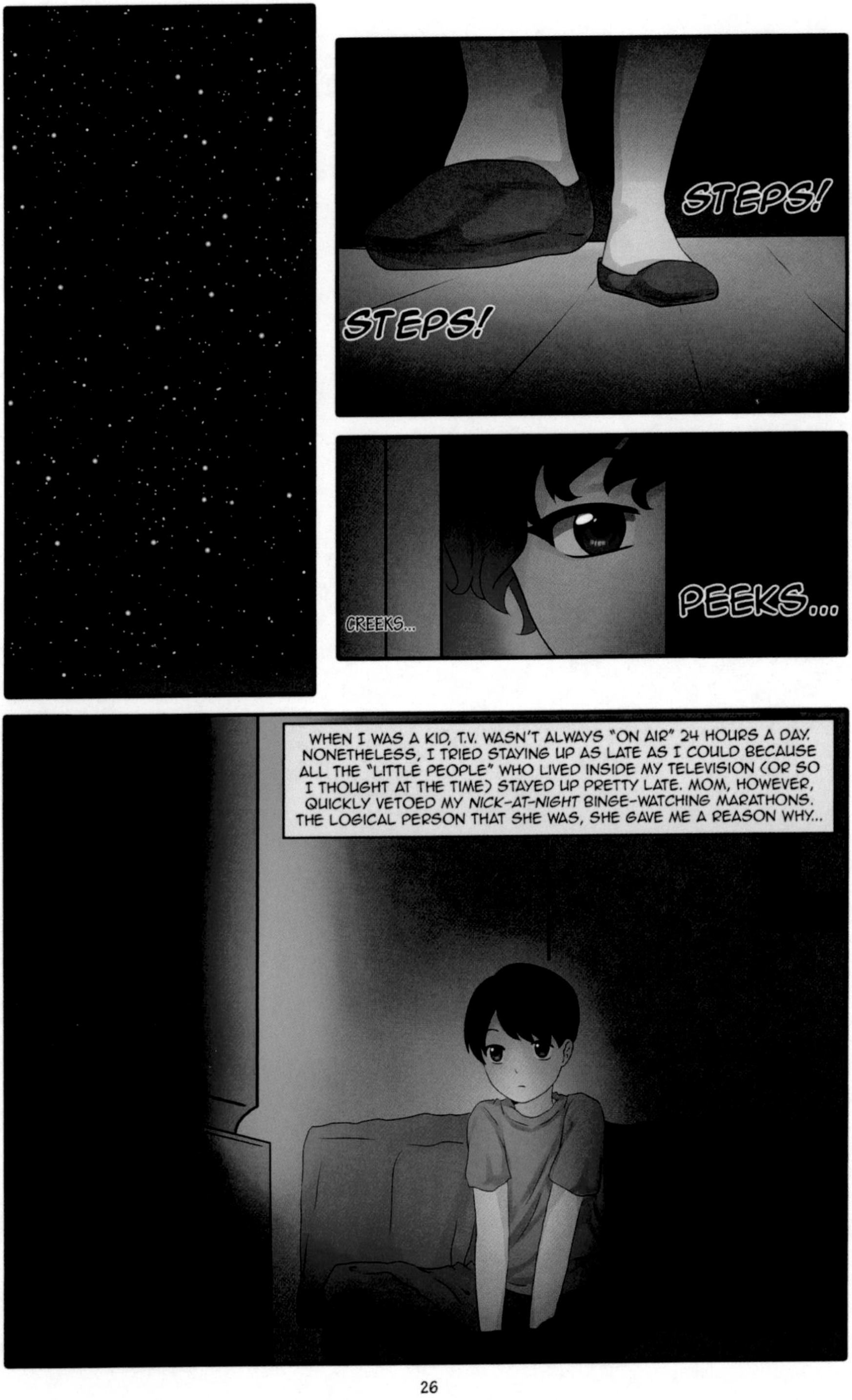
STEPS!
STEPS!
CREEKS...
PEEKS...
WHEN I WAS A KID, T.V. WASN'T ALWAYS "ON AIR" 24 HOURS A DAY. NONETHELESS, I TRIED STAYING UP AS LATE AS I COULD BECAUSE ALL THE "LITTLE PEOPLE" WHO LIVED INSIDE MY TELEVISION (OR SO I THOUGHT AT THE TIME) STAYED UP PRETTY LATE. MOM, HOWEVER, QUICKLY VETOED MY *NICK-AT-NIGHT* BINGE-WATCHING MARATHONS. THE LOGICAL PERSON THAT SHE WAS, SHE GAVE ME A REASON WHY...

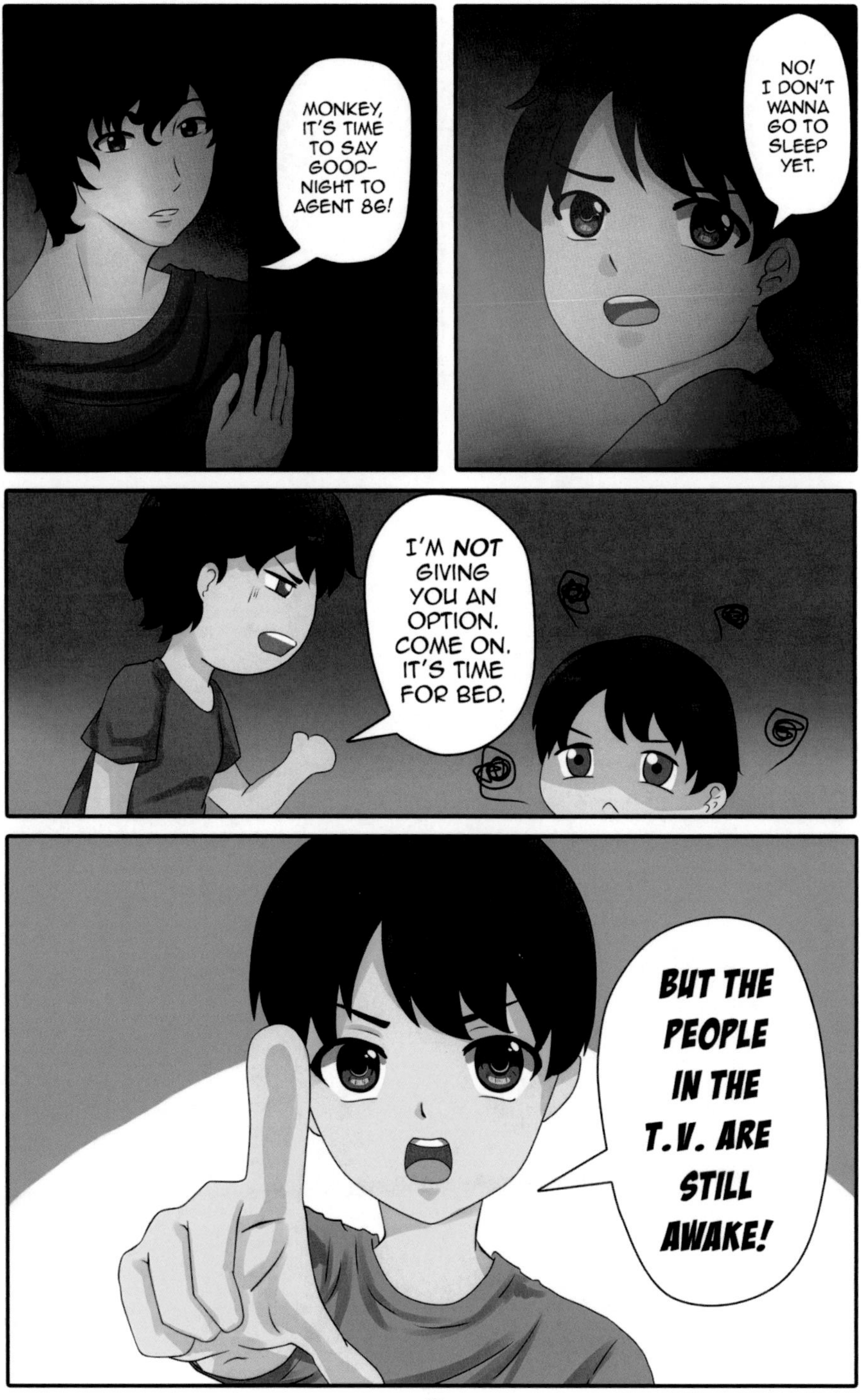
MONKEY, IT'S TIME TO SAY GOOD-NIGHT TO AGENT 86!
NO! I DON'T WANNA GO TO SLEEP YET.
I'M **NOT** GIVING YOU AN OPTION. COME ON. IT'S TIME FOR BED.
BUT THE PEOPLE IN THE T.V. ARE STILL AWAKE!

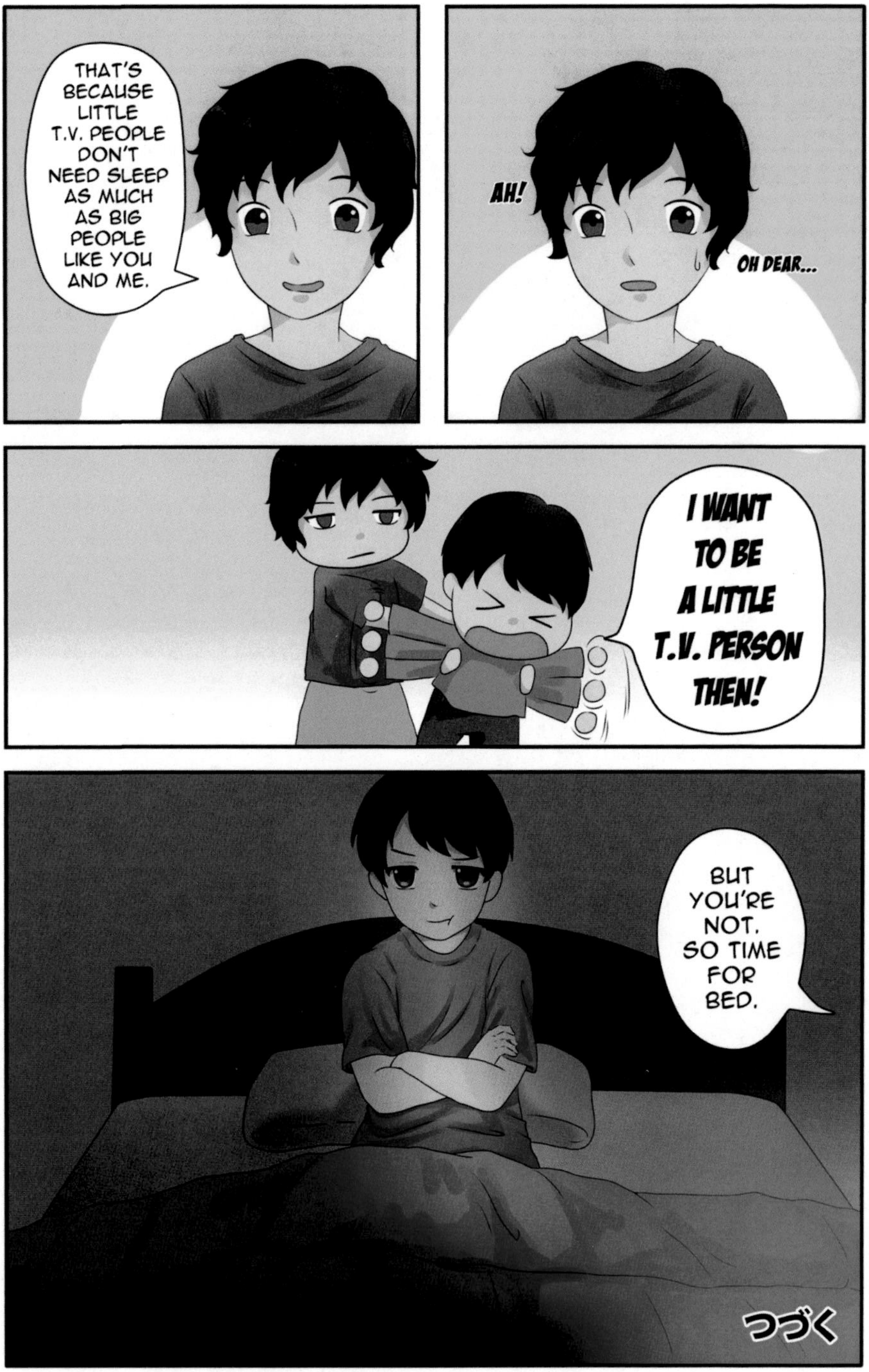
THAT'S BECAUSE LITTLE T.V. PEOPLE DON'T NEED SLEEP AS MUCH AS BIG PEOPLE LIKE YOU AND ME.
AH!
OH DEAR...
I WANT TO BE A LITTLE T.V. PERSON THEN!
BUT YOU'RE NOT. SO TIME FOR BED.
つづく

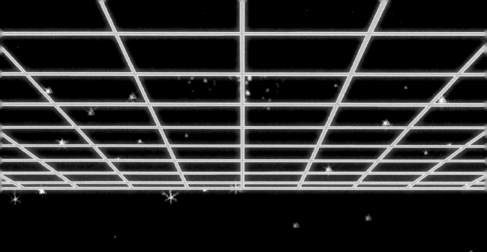

Just Say No!

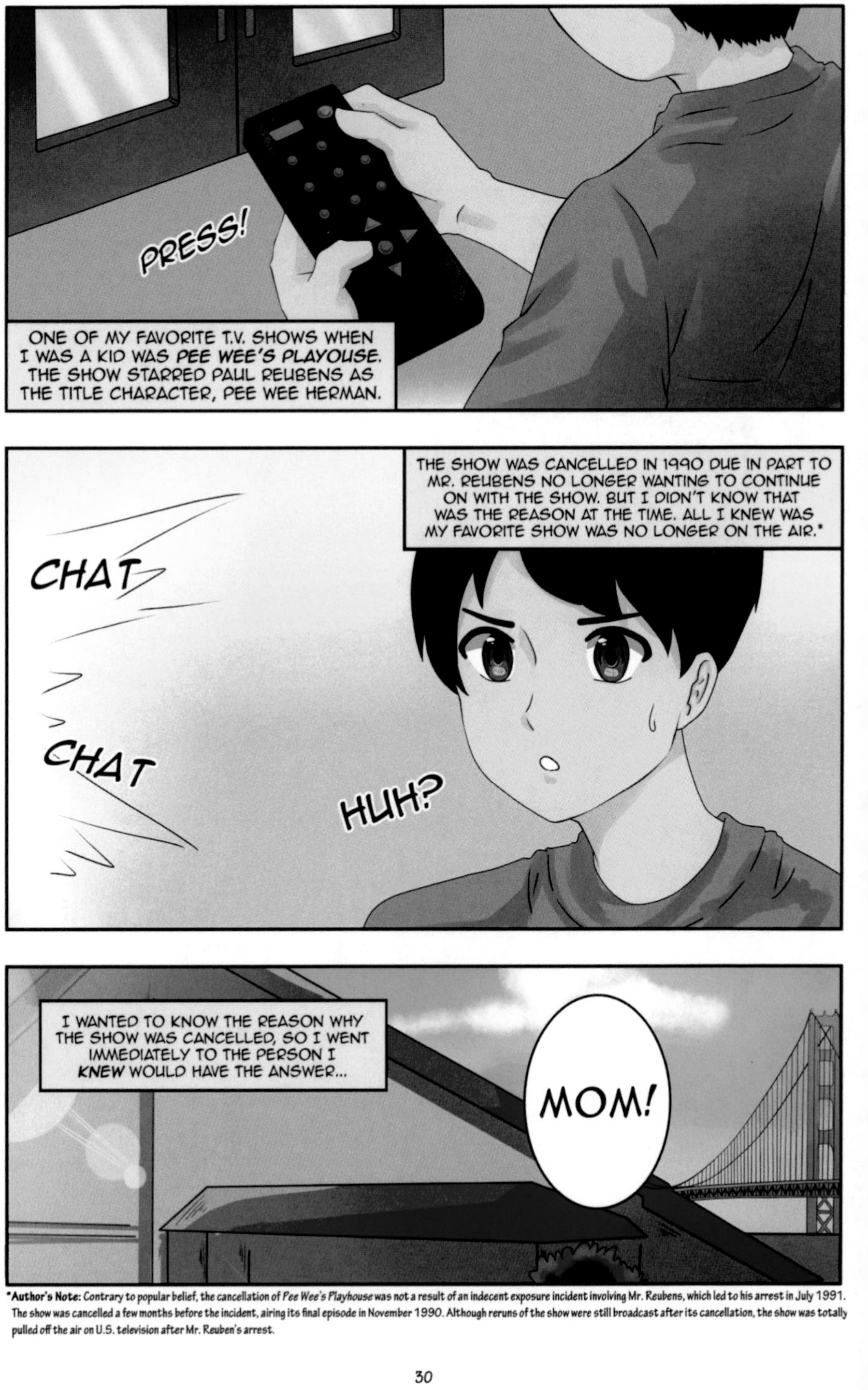
PRESS!
ONE OF MY FAVORITE T.V. SHOWS WHEN I WAS A KID WAS *PEE WEE'S PLAYOUSE*. THE SHOW STARRED PAUL REUBENS AS THE TITLE CHARACTER, PEE WEE HERMAN.
THE SHOW WAS CANCELLED IN 1990 DUE IN PART TO MR. REUBENS NO LONGER WANTING TO CONTINUE ON WITH THE SHOW. BUT I DIDN'T KNOW THAT WAS THE REASON AT THE TIME. ALL I KNEW WAS MY FAVORITE SHOW WAS NO LONGER ON THE AIR.*
CHAT
CHAT
HUH?
I WANTED TO KNOW THE REASON WHY THE SHOW WAS CANCELLED, SO I WENT IMMEDIATELY TO THE PERSON I **KNEW** WOULD HAVE THE ANSWER...
MOM!

***Author's Note:** Contrary to popular belief, the cancellation of *Pee Wee's Playhouse* was not a result of an indecent exposure incident involving Mr. Reubens, which led to his arrest in July 1991. The show was cancelled a few months before the incident, airing its final episode in November 1990. Although reruns of the show were still broadcast after its cancellation, the show was totally pulled off the air on U.S. television after Mr. Reuben's arrest.

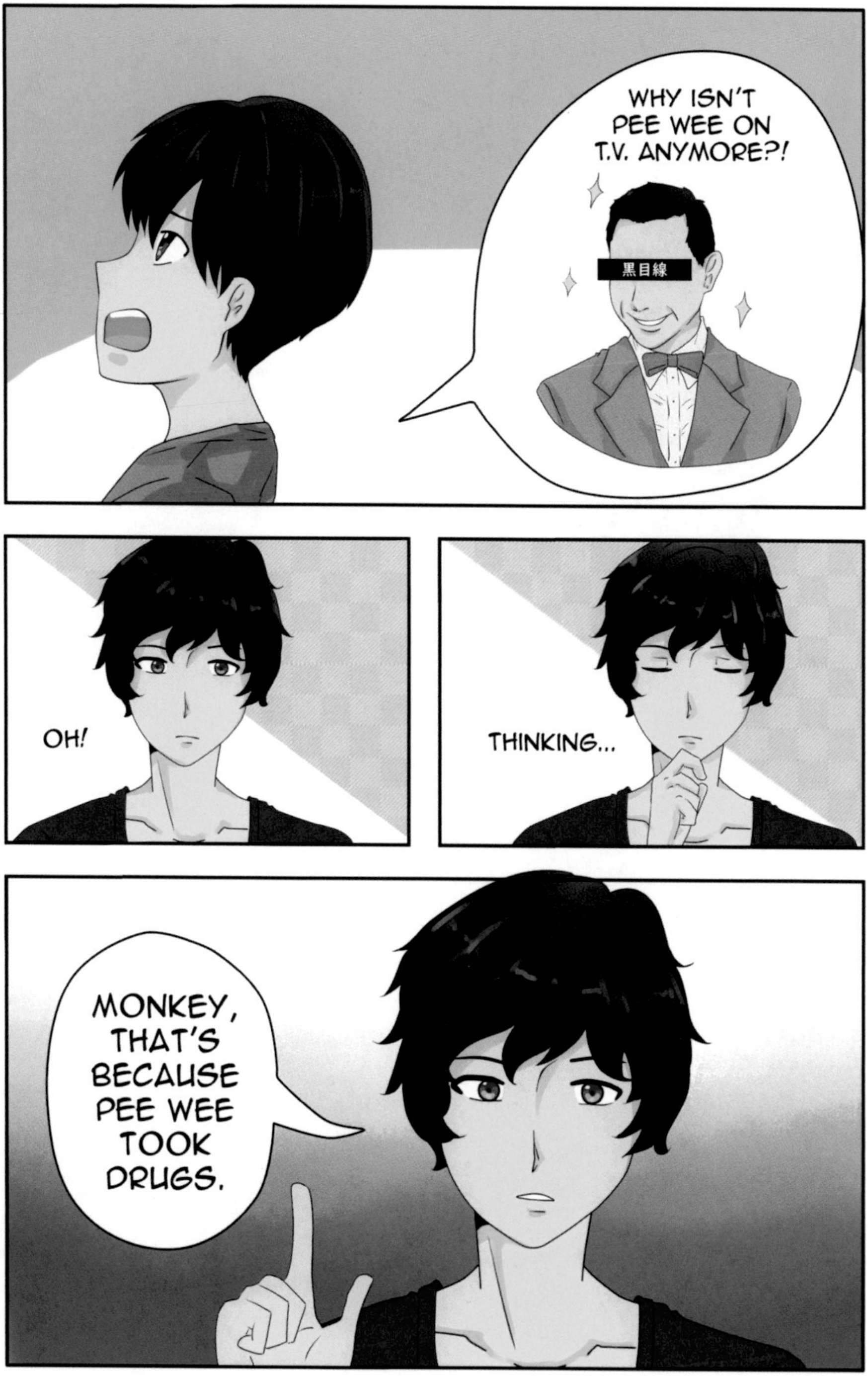
WHY ISN'T PEE WEE ON T.V. ANYMORE?!
黒目線
OH!
THINKING...
MONKEY, THAT'S BECAUSE PEE WEE TOOK DRUGS.

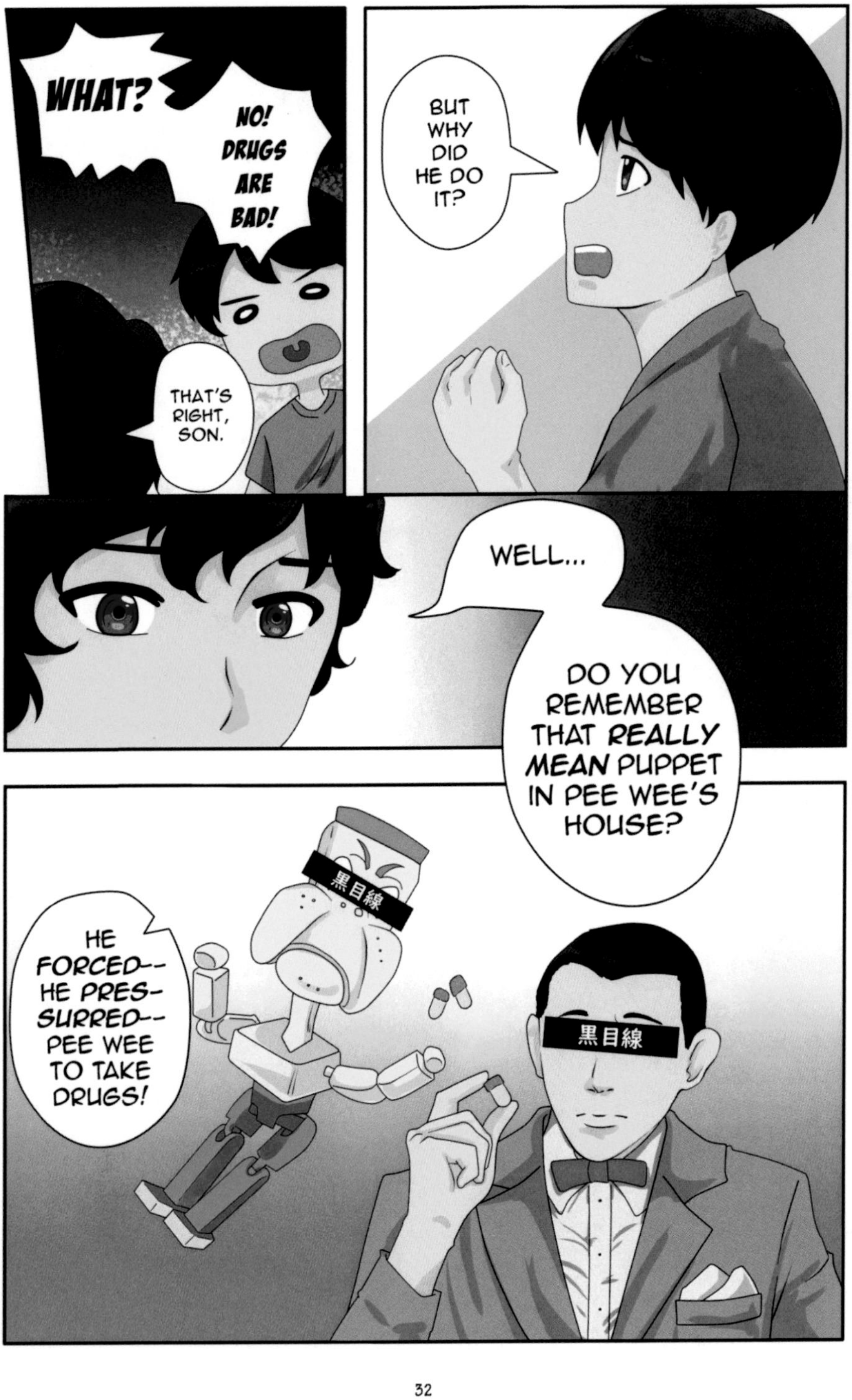
WHAT?
NO! DRUGS ARE BAD!
THAT'S RIGHT, SON.
BUT WHY DID HE DO IT?
WELL...
DO YOU REMEMBER THAT REALLY MEAN PUPPET IN PEE WEE'S HOUSE?
黒目線
HE FORCED-- HE PRES-SURRED-- PEE WEE TO TAKE DRUGS!
黒目線

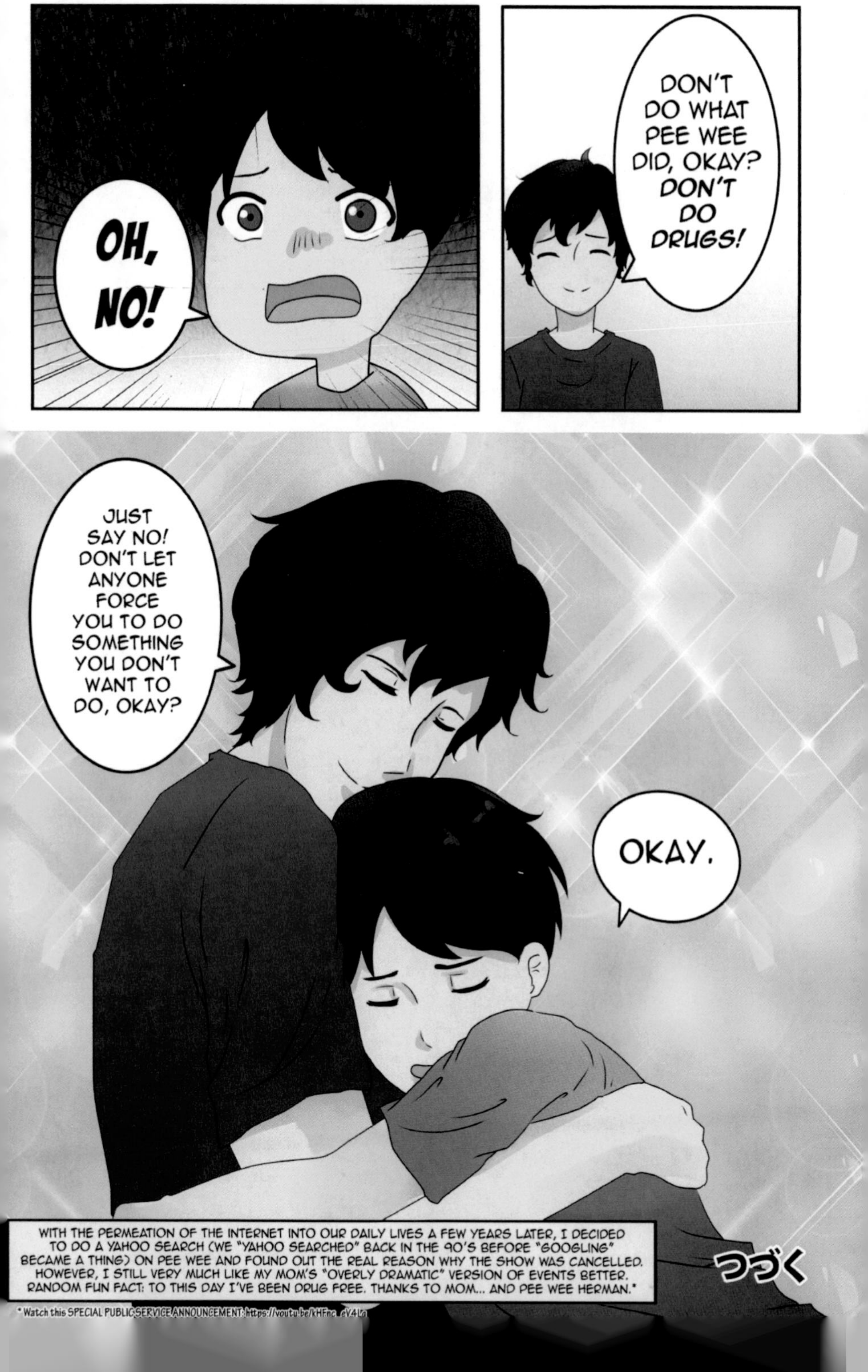
OH, NO!
DON'T DO WHAT PEE WEE DID, OKAY? DON'T DO DRUGS!
JUST SAY NO! DON'T LET ANYONE FORCE YOU TO DO SOMETHING YOU DON'T WANT TO DO, OKAY?
OKAY.
WITH THE PERMEATION OF THE INTERNET INTO OUR DAILY LIVES A FEW YEARS LATER, I DECIDED TO DO A YAHOO SEARCH (WE "YAHOO SEARCHED" BACK IN THE 90'S BEFORE "GOOGLING" BECAME A THING) ON PEE WEE AND FOUND OUT THE REAL REASON WHY THE SHOW WAS CANCELLED. HOWEVER, I STILL VERY MUCH LIKE MY MOM'S "OVERLY DRAMATIC" VERSION OF EVENTS BETTER. RANDOM FUN FACT: TO THIS DAY I'VE BEEN DRUG FREE. THANKS TO MOM... AND PEE WEE HERMAN.*
つづく
* Watch this SPECIAL PUBLIC SERVICE ANNOUNCEMENT: https://youtu.be/kHFnc_eV4La

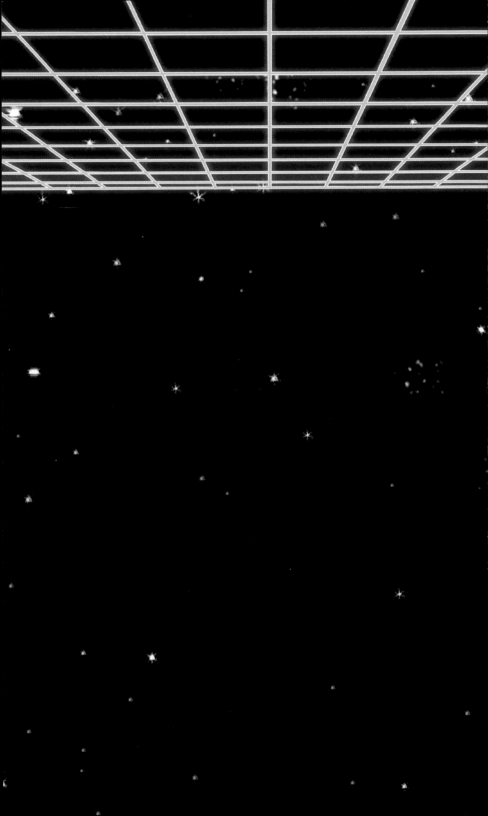

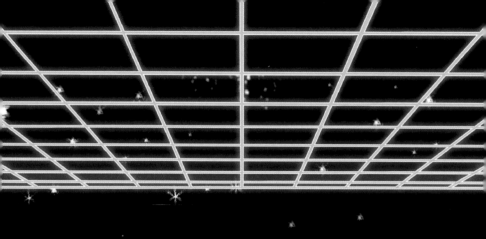

The Birds and the Bees

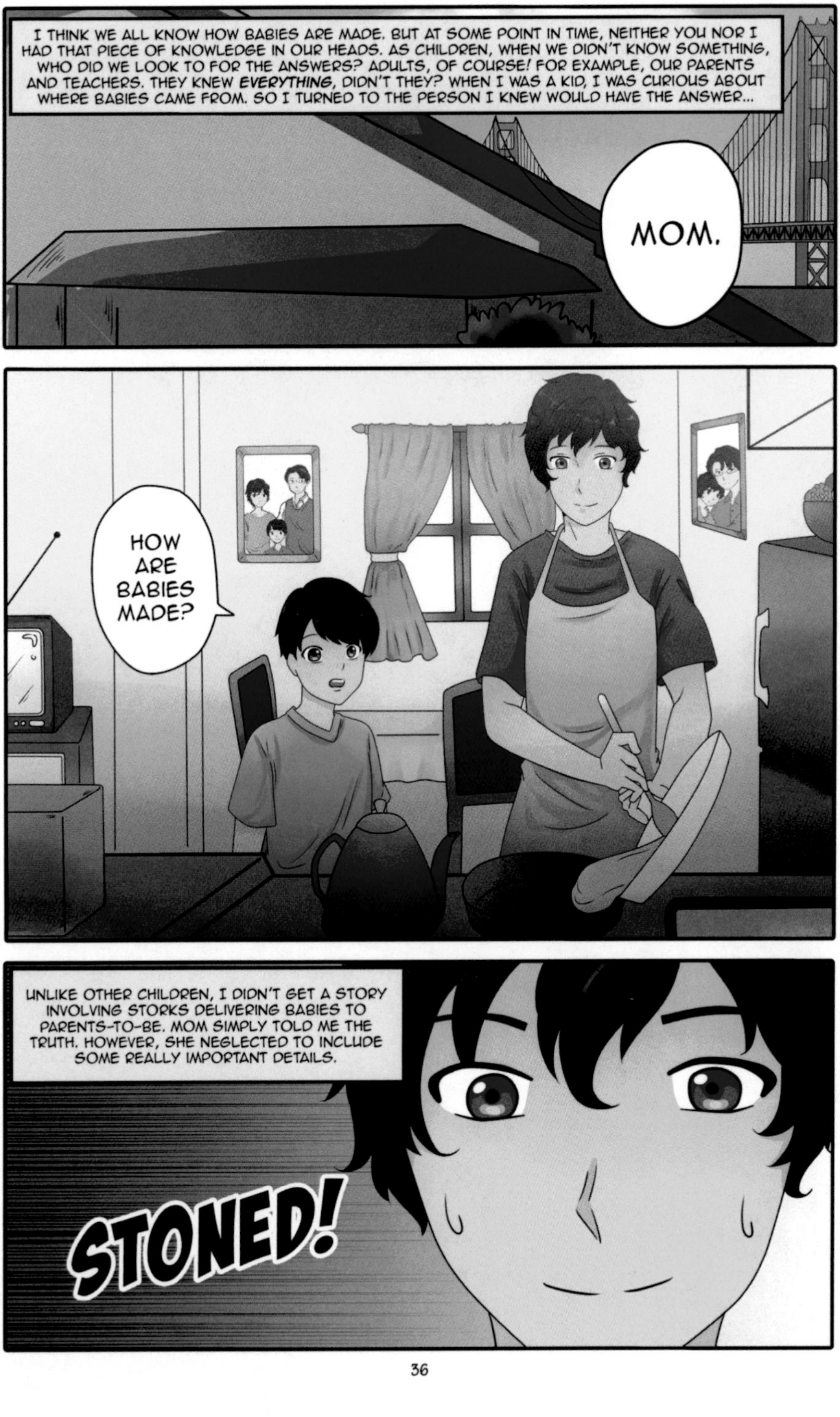

I THINK WE ALL KNOW HOW BABIES ARE MADE. BUT AT SOME POINT IN TIME, NEITHER YOU NOR I HAD THAT PIECE OF KNOWLEDGE IN OUR HEADS. AS CHILDREN, WHEN WE DIDN'T KNOW SOMETHING, WHO DID WE LOOK TO FOR THE ANSWERS? ADULTS, OF COURSE! FOR EXAMPLE, OUR PARENTS AND TEACHERS. THEY KNEW *EVERYTHING*, DIDN'T THEY? WHEN I WAS A KID, I WAS CURIOUS ABOUT WHERE BABIES CAME FROM. SO I TURNED TO THE PERSON I KNEW WOULD HAVE THE ANSWER...
MOM.
HOW ARE BABIES MADE?
UNLIKE OTHER CHILDREN, I DIDN'T GET A STORY INVOLVING STORKS DELIVERING BABIES TO PARENTS-TO-BE. MOM SIMPLY TOLD ME THE TRUTH. HOWEVER, SHE NEGLECTED TO INCLUDE SOME REALLY IMPORTANT DETAILS.
STONED!

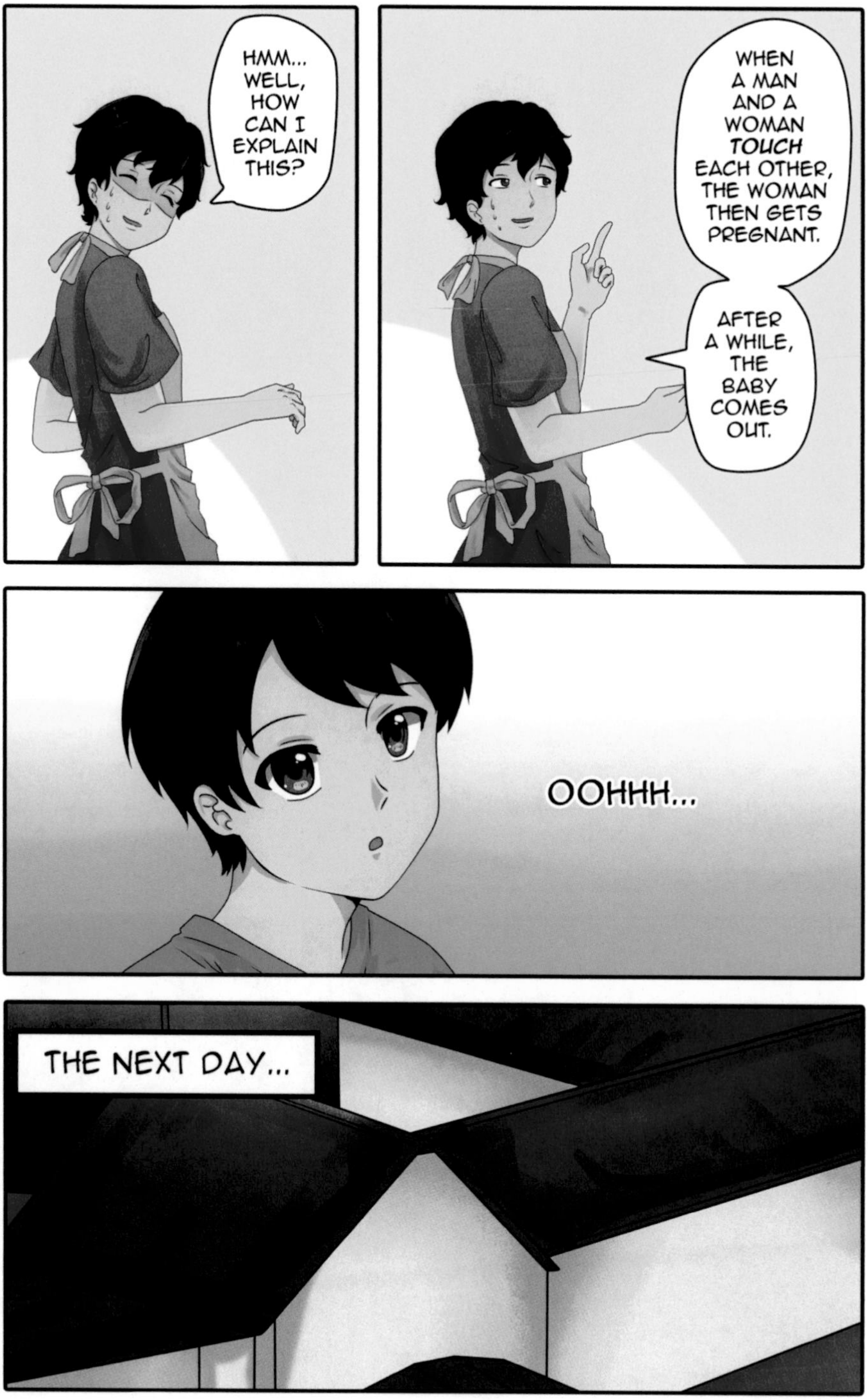
HMM... WELL, HOW CAN I EXPLAIN THIS?
WHEN A MAN AND A WOMAN **TOUCH** EACH OTHER, THE WOMAN THEN GETS PREGNANT.
AFTER A WHILE, THE BABY COMES OUT.
OOHHH...
THE NEXT DAY...

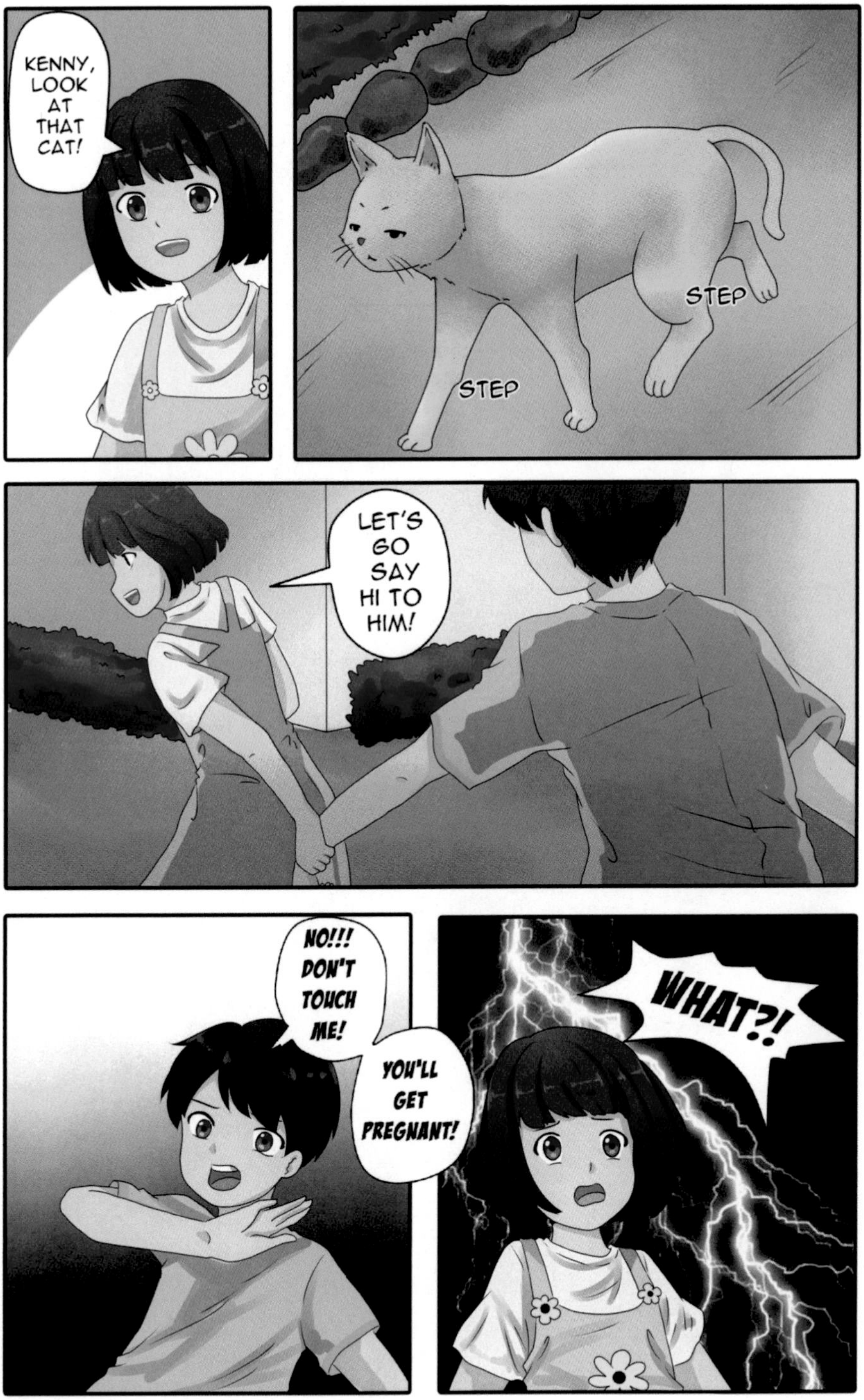
KENNY, LOOK AT THAT CAT!
STEP
STEP
LET'S GO SAY HI TO HIM!
NO!!! DON'T TOUCH ME!
YOU'LL GET PREGNANT!
WHAT?!

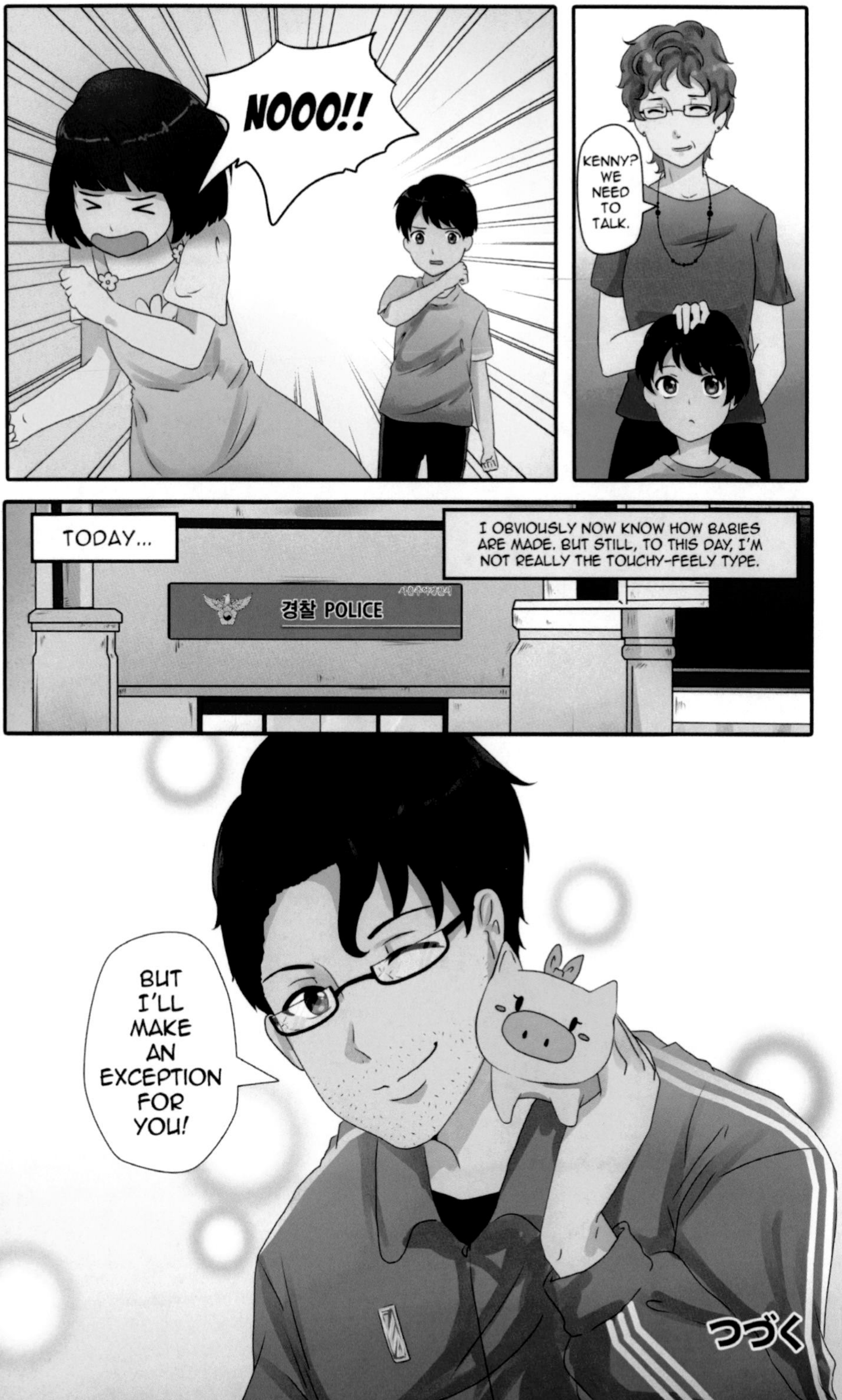

NOOO!!
KENNY? WE NEED TO TALK.
TODAY...
I OBVIOUSLY NOW KNOW HOW BABIES ARE MADE. BUT STILL, TO THIS DAY, I'M NOT REALLY THE TOUCHY-FEELY TYPE.
경찰 POLICE
BUT I'LL MAKE AN EXCEPTION FOR YOU!
つづく

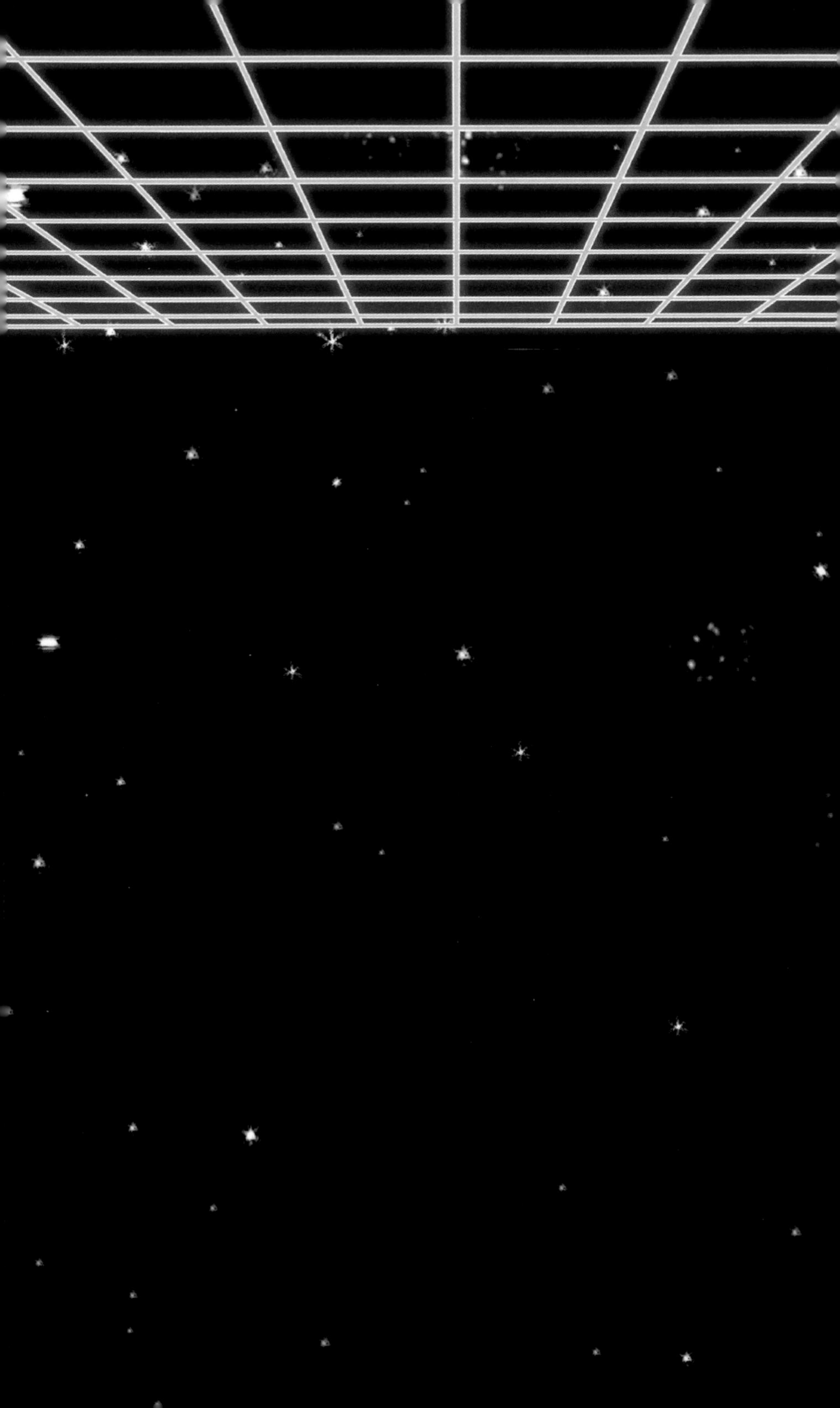

There is No Shrimp

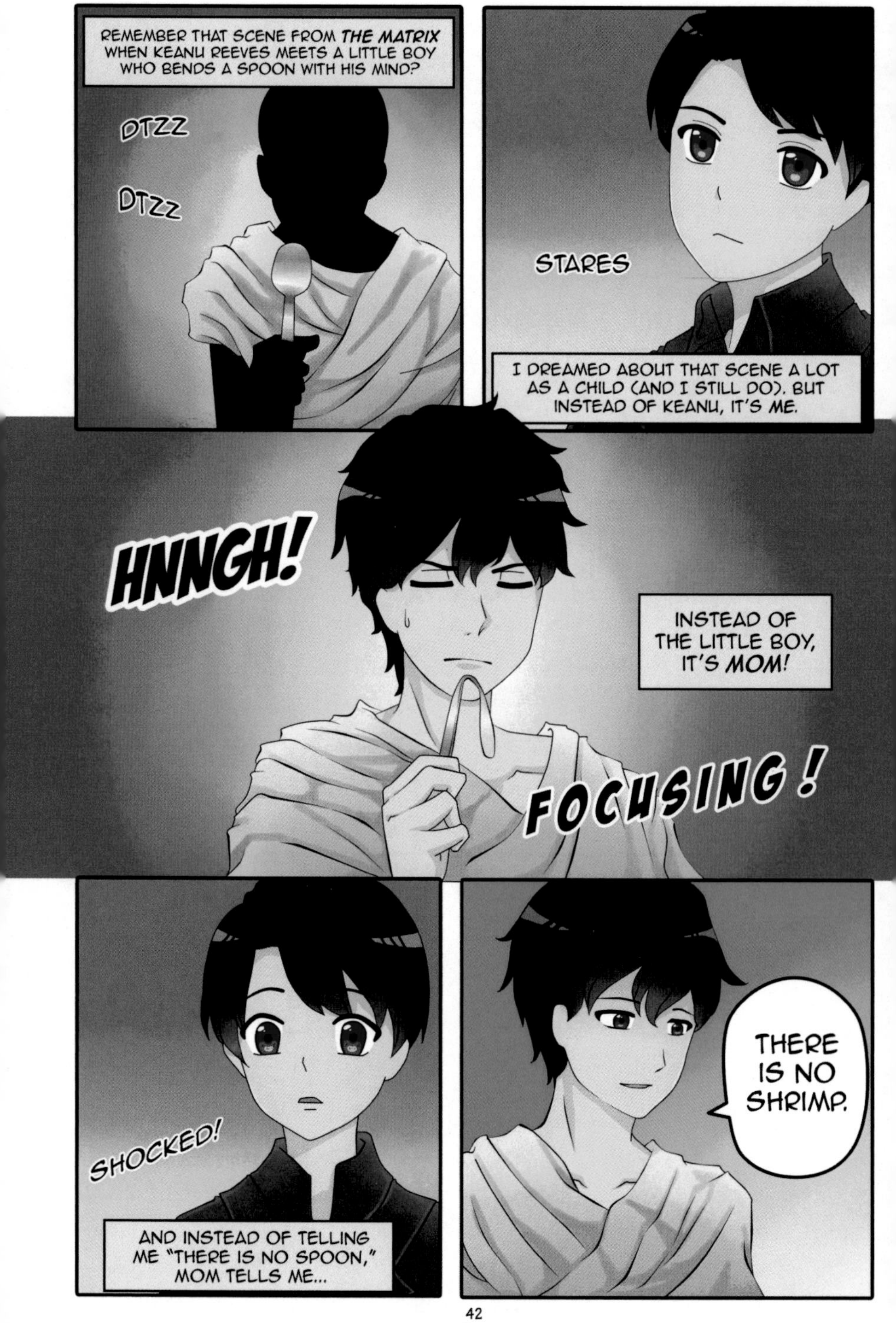
REMEMBER THAT SCENE FROM *THE MATRIX* WHEN KEANU REEVES MEETS A LITTLE BOY WHO BENDS A SPOON WITH HIS MIND?
DTZZ
DTZZ
STARES
I DREAMED ABOUT THAT SCENE A LOT AS A CHILD (AND I STILL DO). BUT INSTEAD OF KEANU, IT'S *ME*.
HNNGH!
INSTEAD OF THE LITTLE BOY, IT'S *MOM!*
FOCUSING!
SHOCKED!
AND INSTEAD OF TELLING ME "THERE IS NO SPOON," MOM TELLS ME...
THERE IS NO SHRIMP.

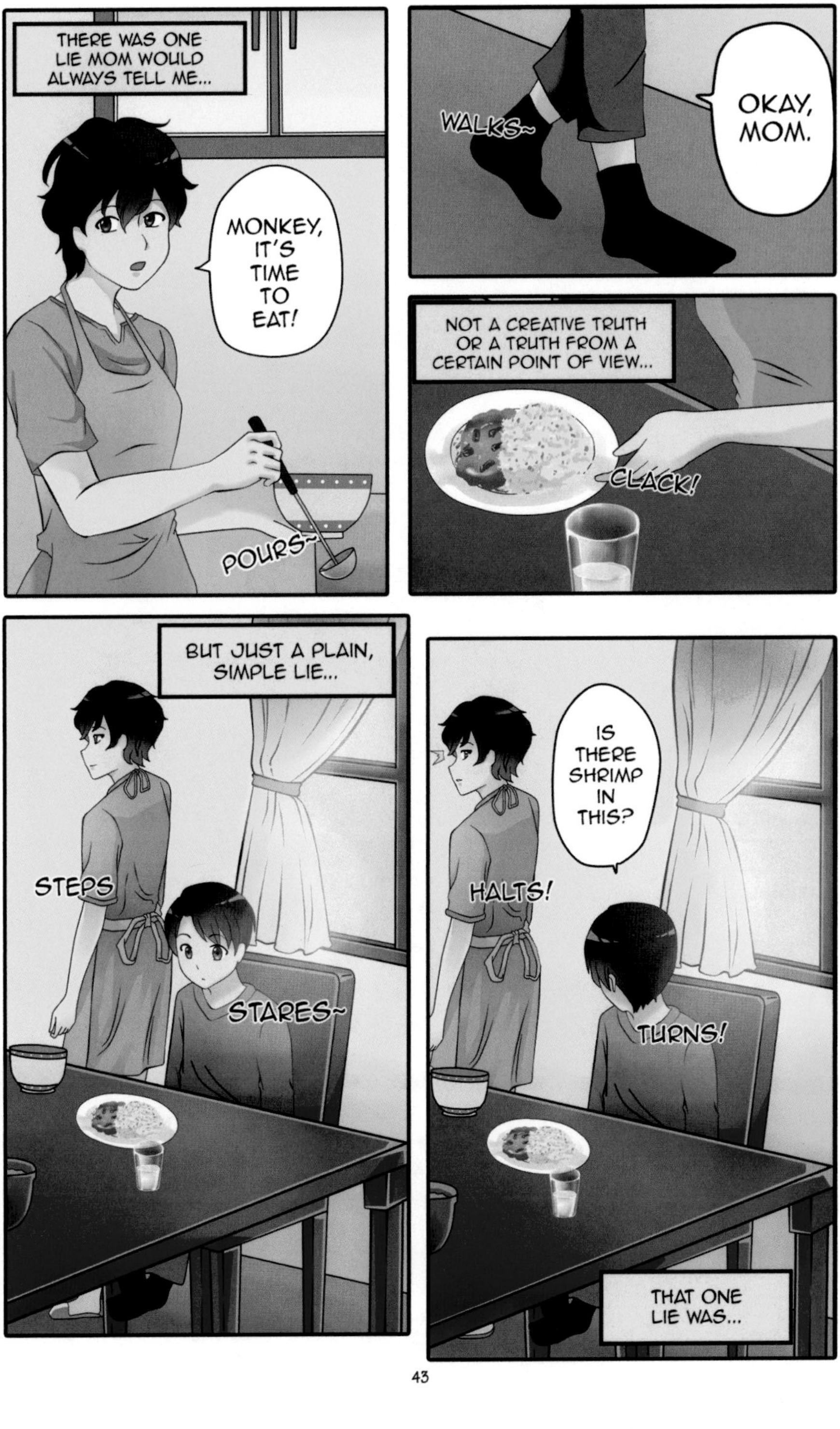
THERE WAS ONE LIE MOM WOULD ALWAYS TELL ME...
MONKEY, IT'S TIME TO EAT!
POURS~
WALKS~
OKAY, MOM.
NOT A CREATIVE TRUTH OR A TRUTH FROM A CERTAIN POINT OF VIEW...
CLACK!
BUT JUST A PLAIN, SIMPLE LIE...
STEPS
STARES~
IS THERE SHRIMP IN THIS?
HALTS!
TURNS!
THAT ONE LIE WAS...

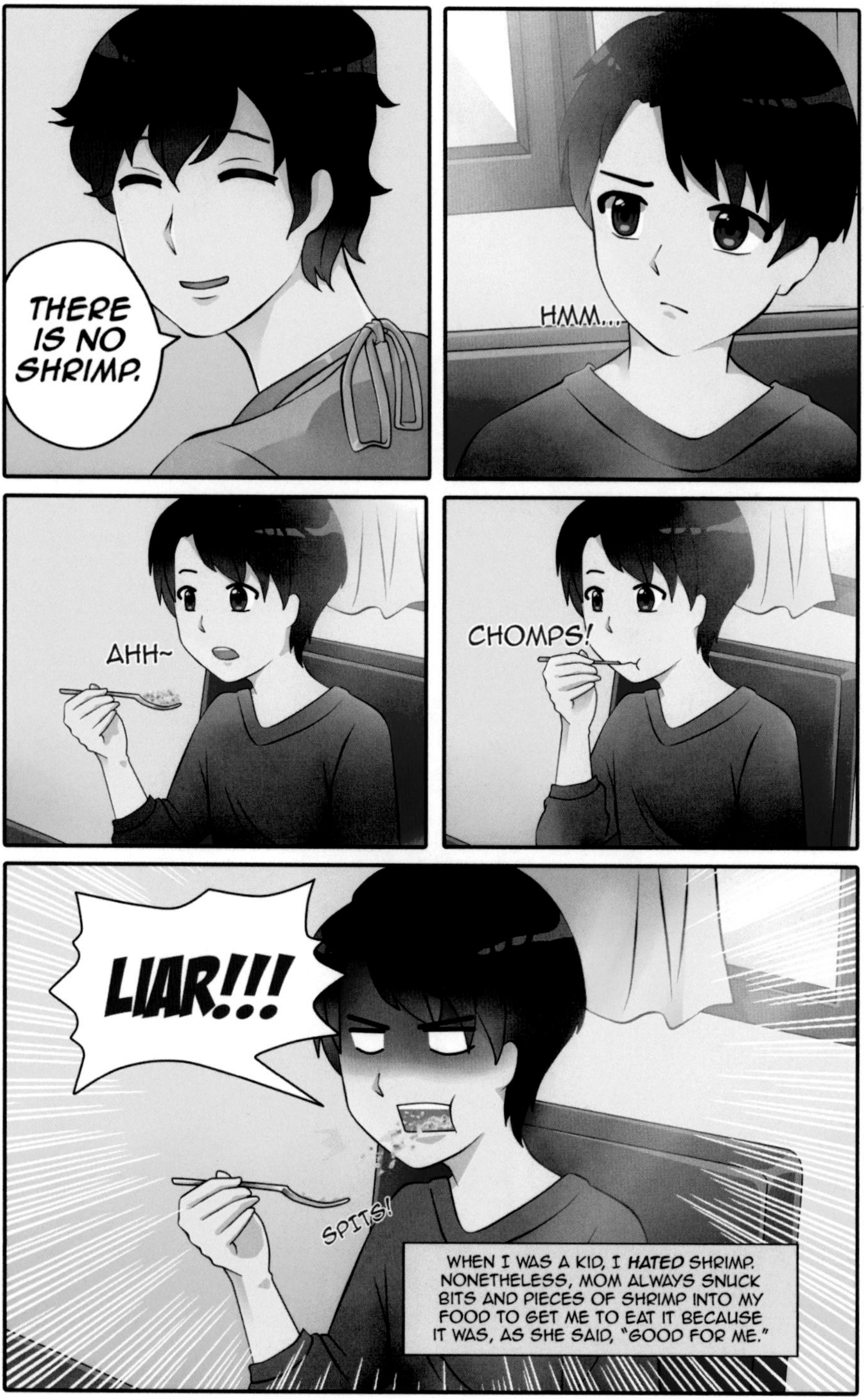
THERE IS NO SHRIMP.
HMM...
AHH~
CHOMPS!
LIAR!!!
SPITS!
WHEN I WAS A KID, I HATED SHRIMP. NONETHELESS, MOM ALWAYS SNUCK BITS AND PIECES OF SHRIMP INTO MY FOOD TO GET ME TO EAT IT BECAUSE IT WAS, AS SHE SAID, "GOOD FOR ME."

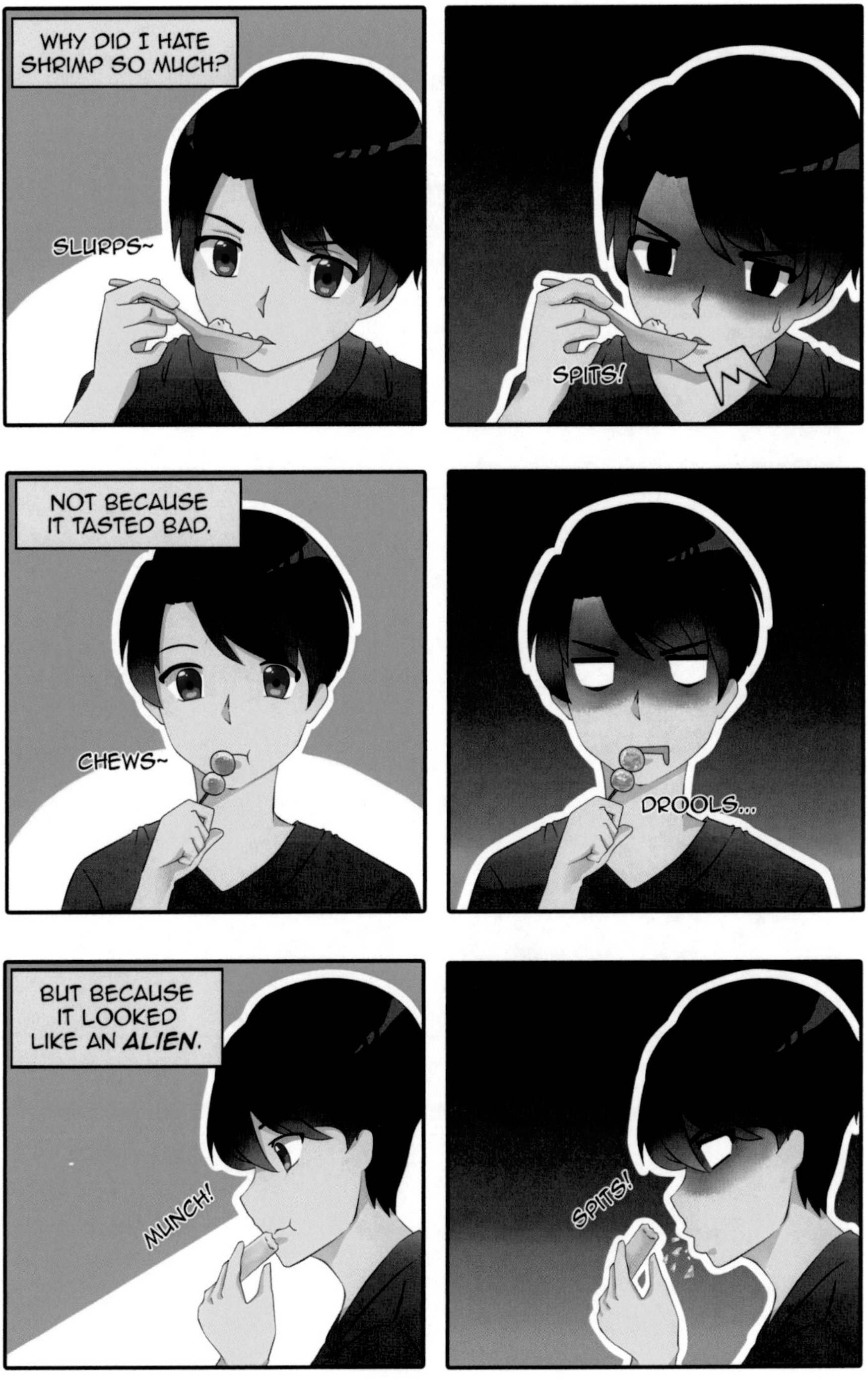
WHY DID I HATE SHRIMP SO MUCH?
SLURPS~
SPITS!
NOT BECAUSE IT TASTED BAD.
CHEWS~
DROOLS...
BUT BECAUSE IT LOOKED LIKE AN *ALIEN*.
MUNCH!
SPITS!

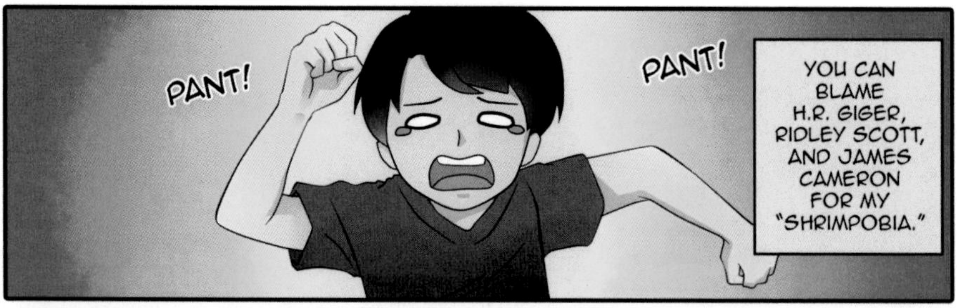
YOU CAN BLAME H.R. GIGER, RIDLEY SCOTT, AND JAMES CAMERON FOR MY "SHRIMPOBIA."
PANT!
PANT!

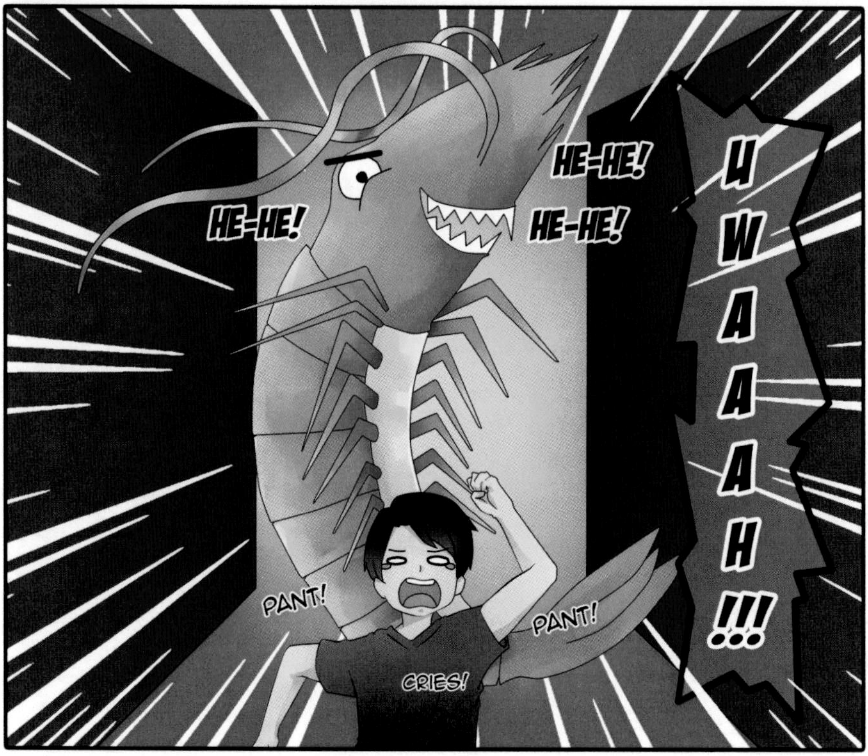
UWAAAAH!!!
HE-HE!
HE-HE!
HE-HE!
PANT!
PANT!
CRIES!

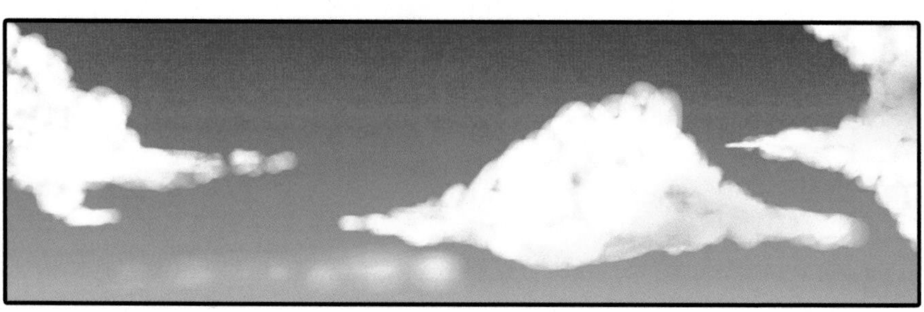

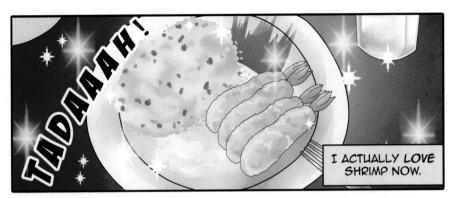

TADAAAH!

I ACTUALLY LOVE SHRIMP NOW.

BUT I DON'T KNOW HOW THE SHRIMPS FEEL ABOUT MY CHANGE OF HEART.

AHH~

CRIES!

CHEWS~

CHUCKLES!

つづく

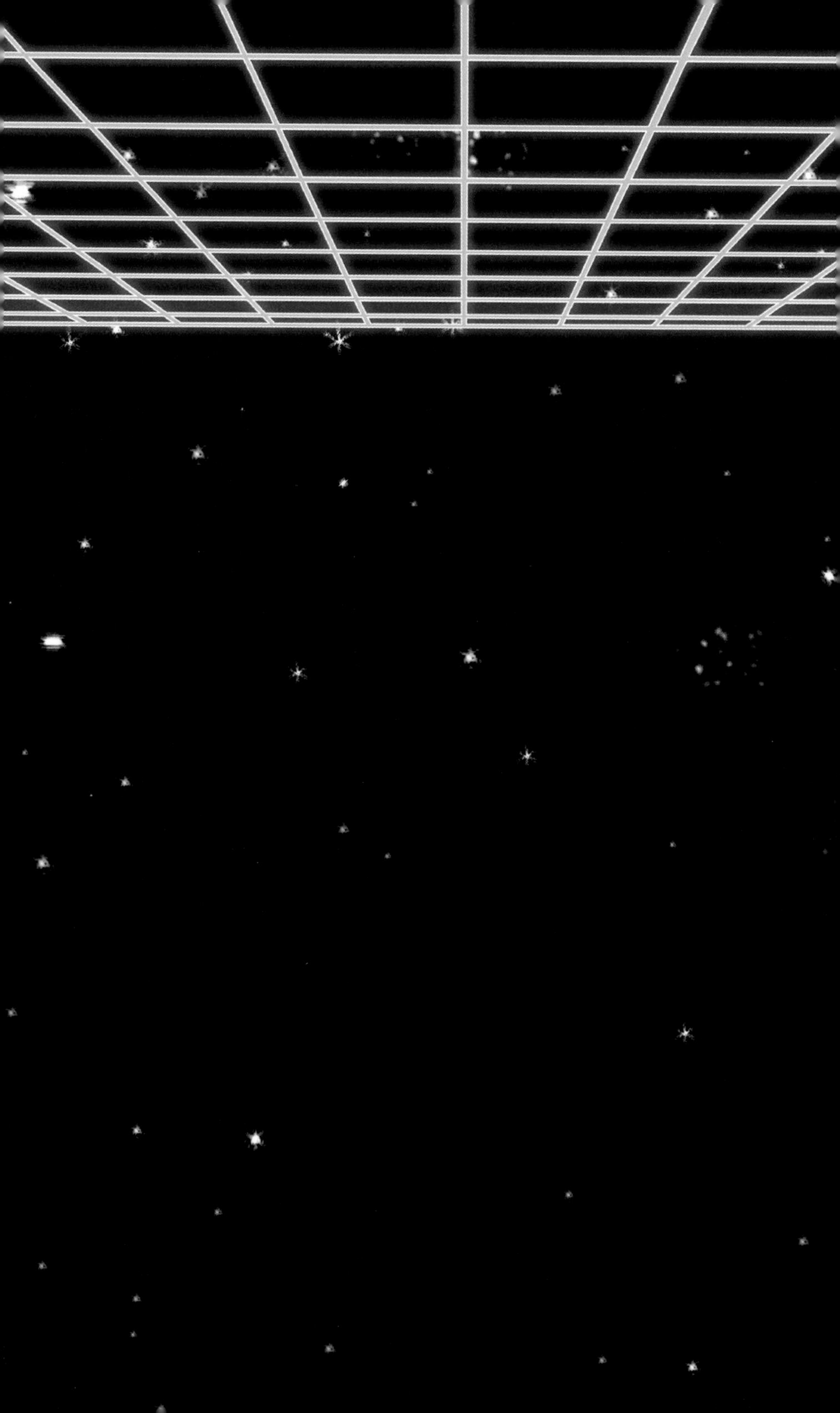

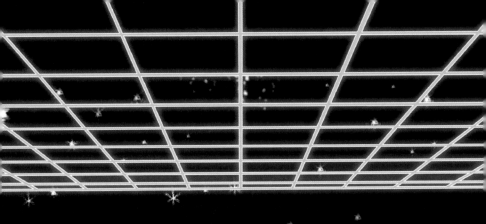

I Love You, Tooth Fairy

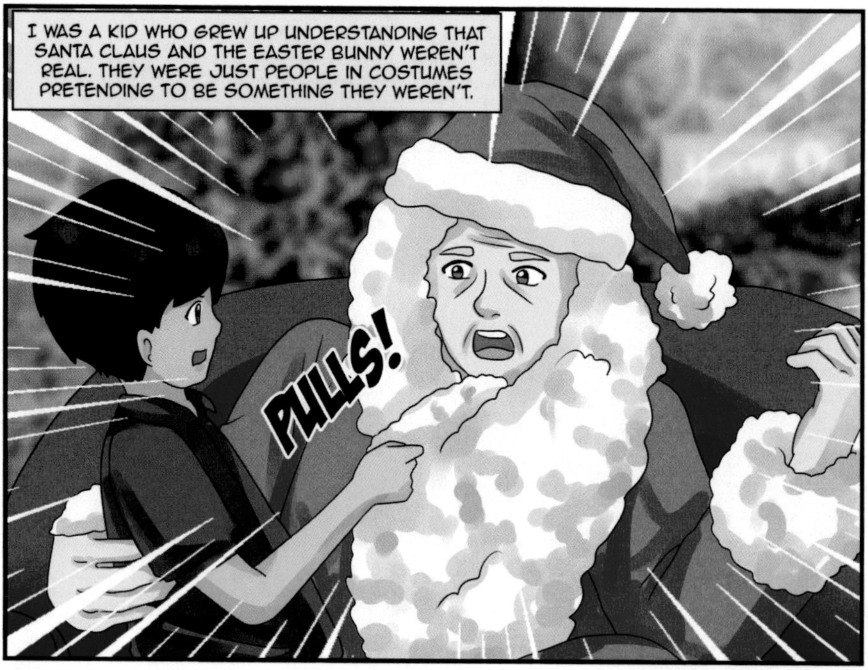
I WAS A KID WHO GREW UP UNDERSTANDING THAT SANTA CLAUS AND THE EASTER BUNNY WEREN'T REAL. THEY WERE JUST PEOPLE IN COSTUMES PRETENDING TO BE SOMETHING THEY WEREN'T.
PULLS!

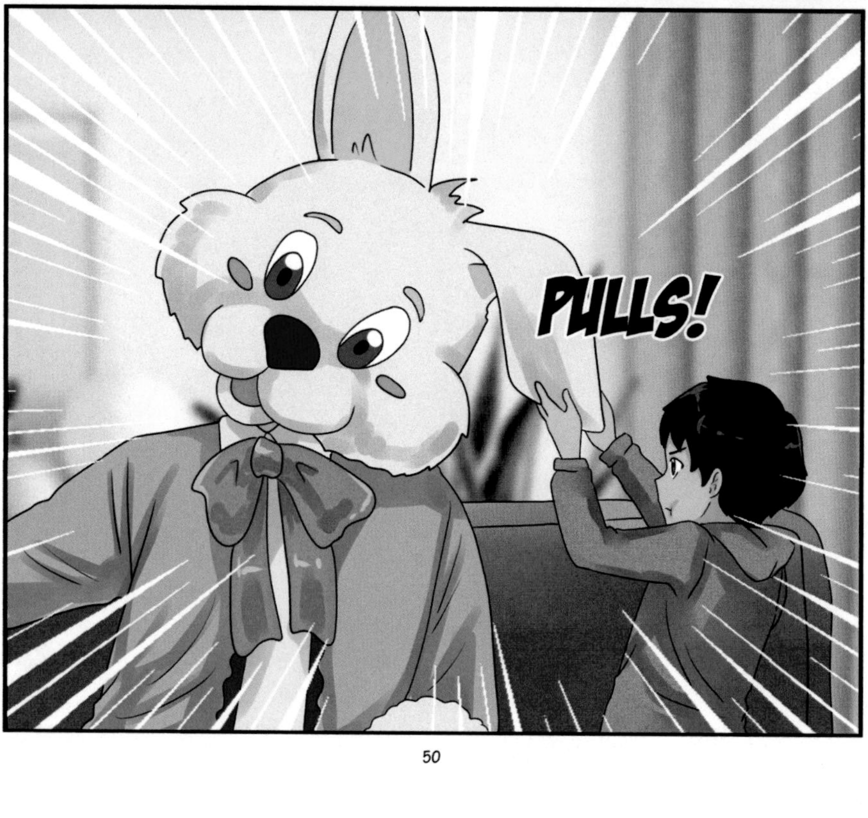
PULLS!

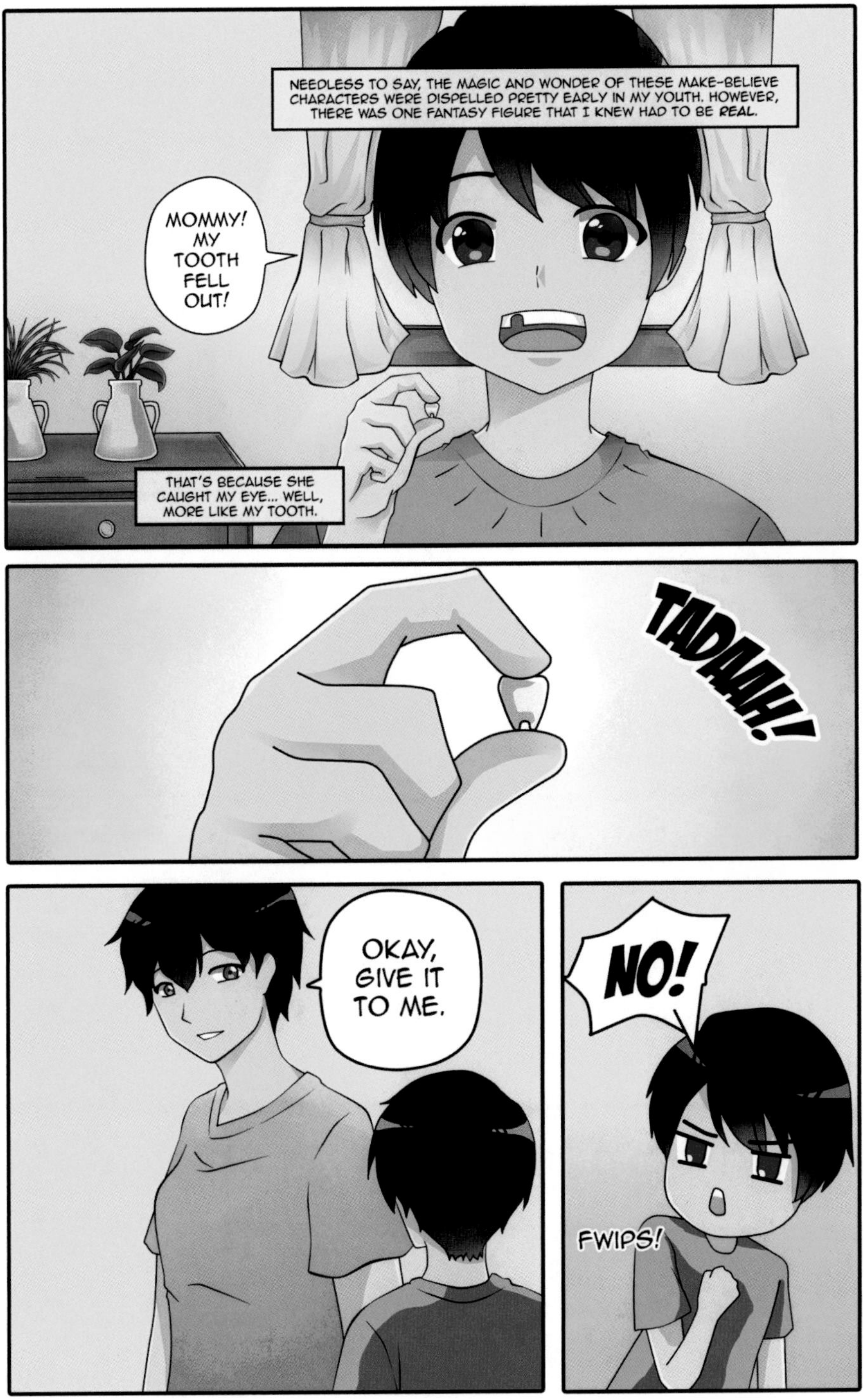
NEEDLESS TO SAY, THE MAGIC AND WONDER OF THESE MAKE-BELIEVE CHARACTERS WERE DISPELLED PRETTY EARLY IN MY YOUTH. HOWEVER, THERE WAS ONE FANTASY FIGURE THAT I KNEW HAD TO BE *REAL*.
MOMMY! MY TOOTH FELL OUT!
THAT'S BECAUSE SHE CAUGHT MY EYE... WELL, MORE LIKE MY TOOTH.
TADAAH!
OKAY, GIVE IT TO ME.
NO!
FWIPS!

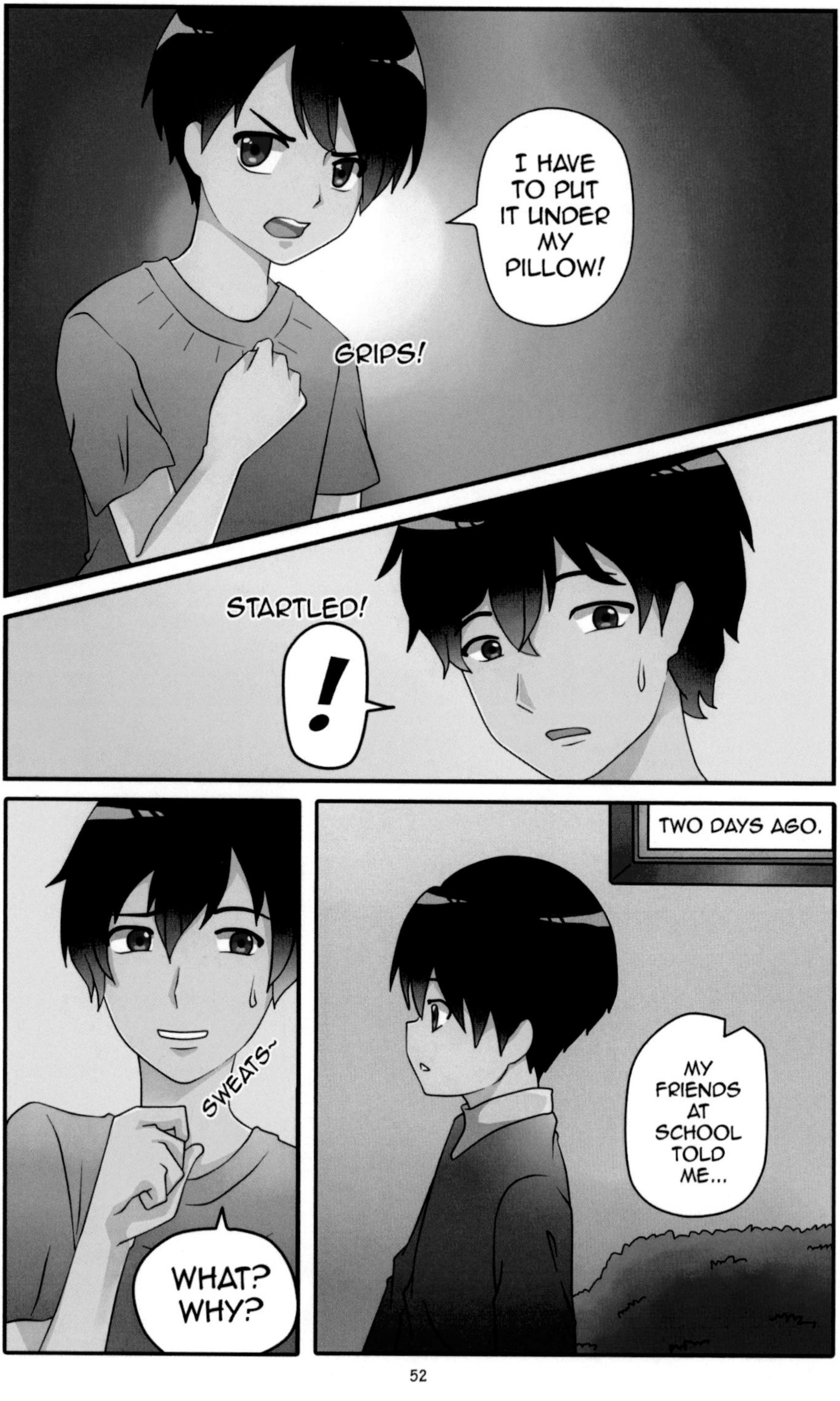
I HAVE TO PUT IT UNDER MY PILLOW!
GRIPS!
STARTLED!
!
SWEATS~
WHAT? WHY?
TWO DAYS AGO.
MY FRIENDS AT SCHOOL TOLD ME...

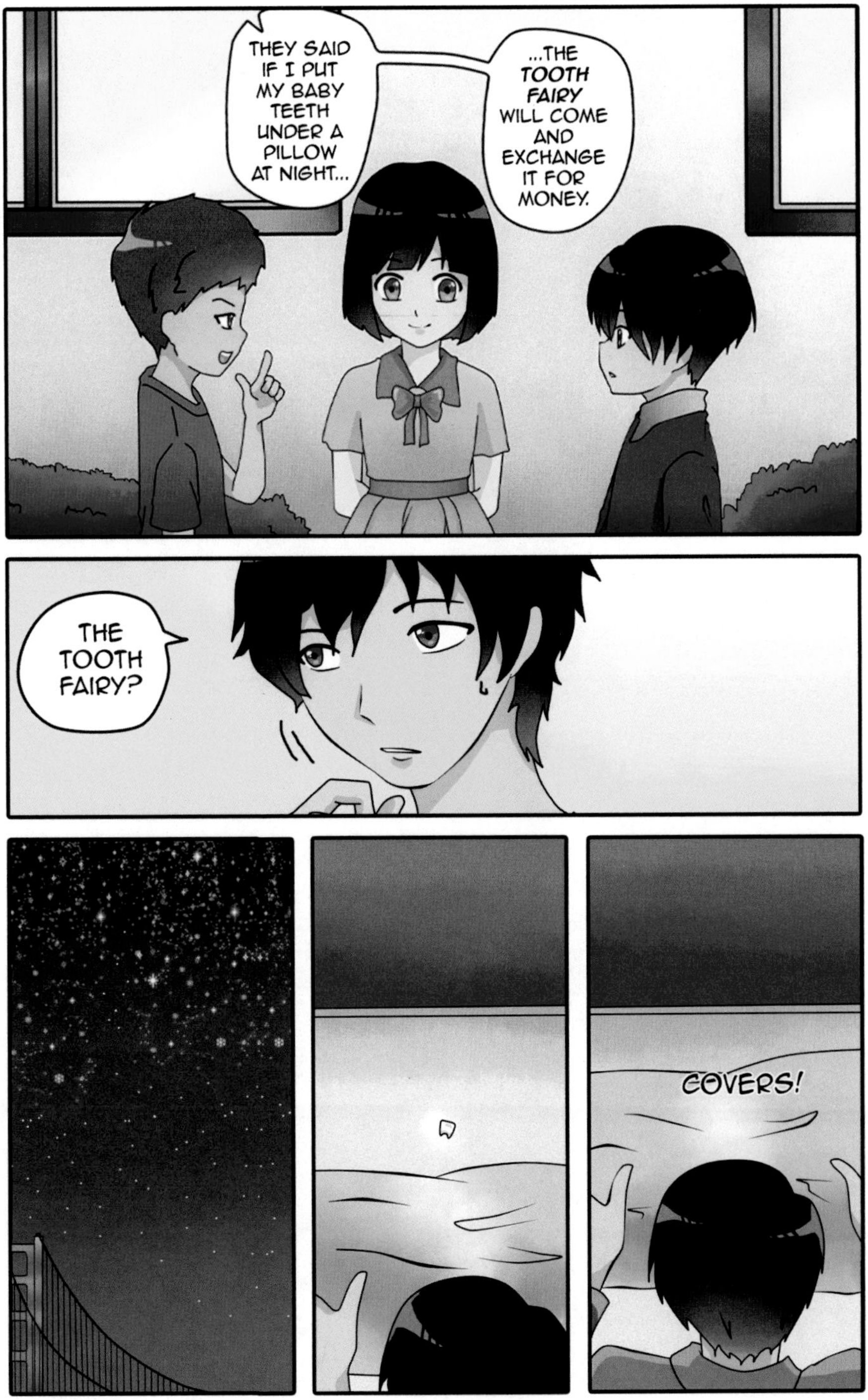
THEY SAID IF I PUT MY BABY TEETH UNDER A PILLOW AT NIGHT...
...THE TOOTH FAIRY WILL COME AND EXCHANGE IT FOR MONEY.
THE TOOTH FAIRY?
COVERS!

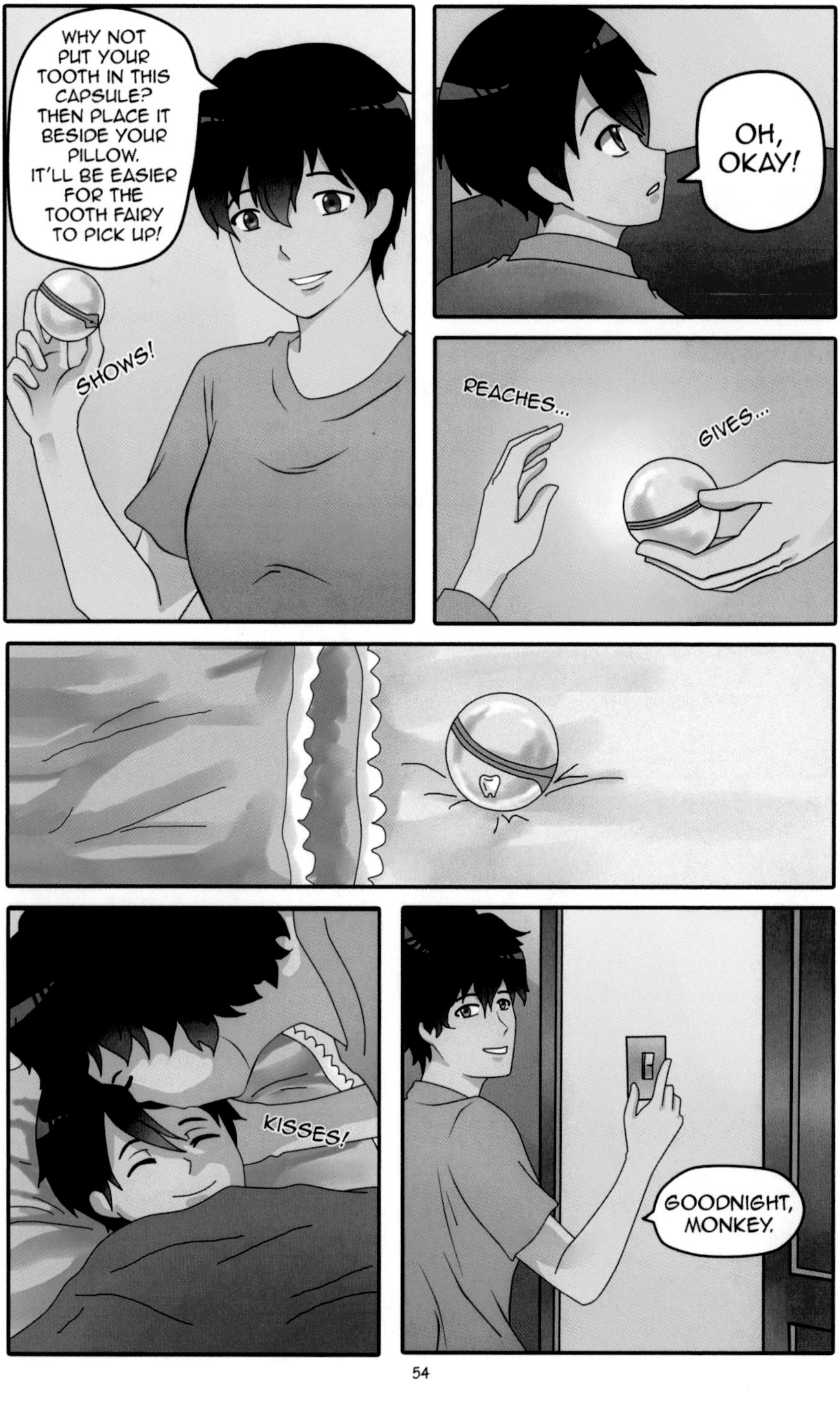

WHY NOT PUT YOUR TOOTH IN THIS CAPSULE? THEN PLACE IT BESIDE YOUR PILLOW. IT'LL BE EASIER FOR THE TOOTH FAIRY TO PICK UP!
SHOWS!
OH, OKAY!
REACHES...
GIVES...
KISSES!
GOODNIGHT, MONKEY.

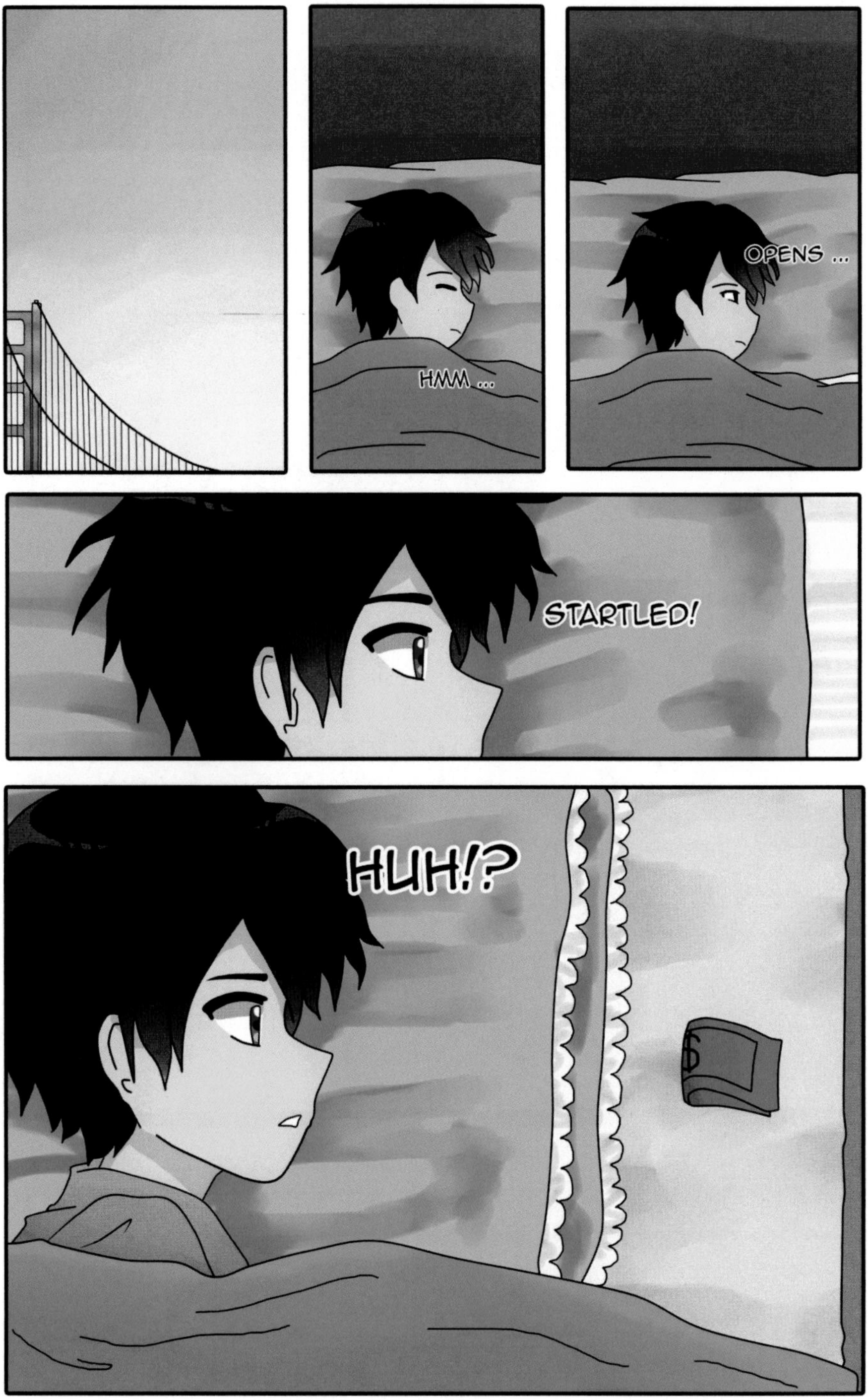
HMM ...
OPENS ...
STARTLED!
HUH!?

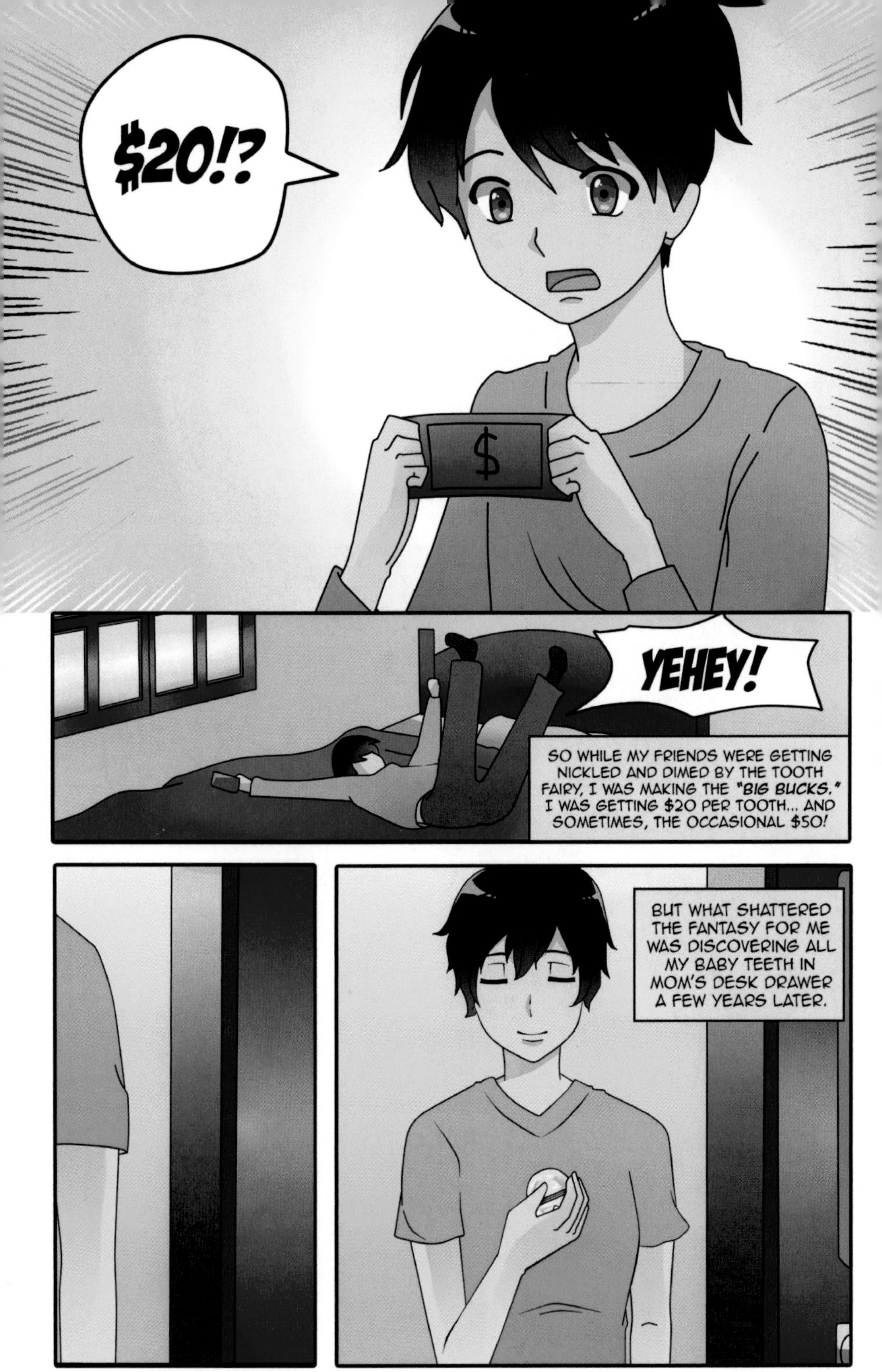

$20!?
YEHEY!
SO WHILE MY FRIENDS WERE GETTING NICKLED AND DIMED BY THE TOOTH FAIRY, I WAS MAKING THE *"BIG BUCKS."* I WAS GETTING $20 PER TOOTH... AND SOMETIMES, THE OCCASIONAL $50!
BUT WHAT SHATTERED THE FANTASY FOR ME WAS DISCOVERING ALL MY BABY TEETH IN MOM'S DESK DRAWER A FEW YEARS LATER.

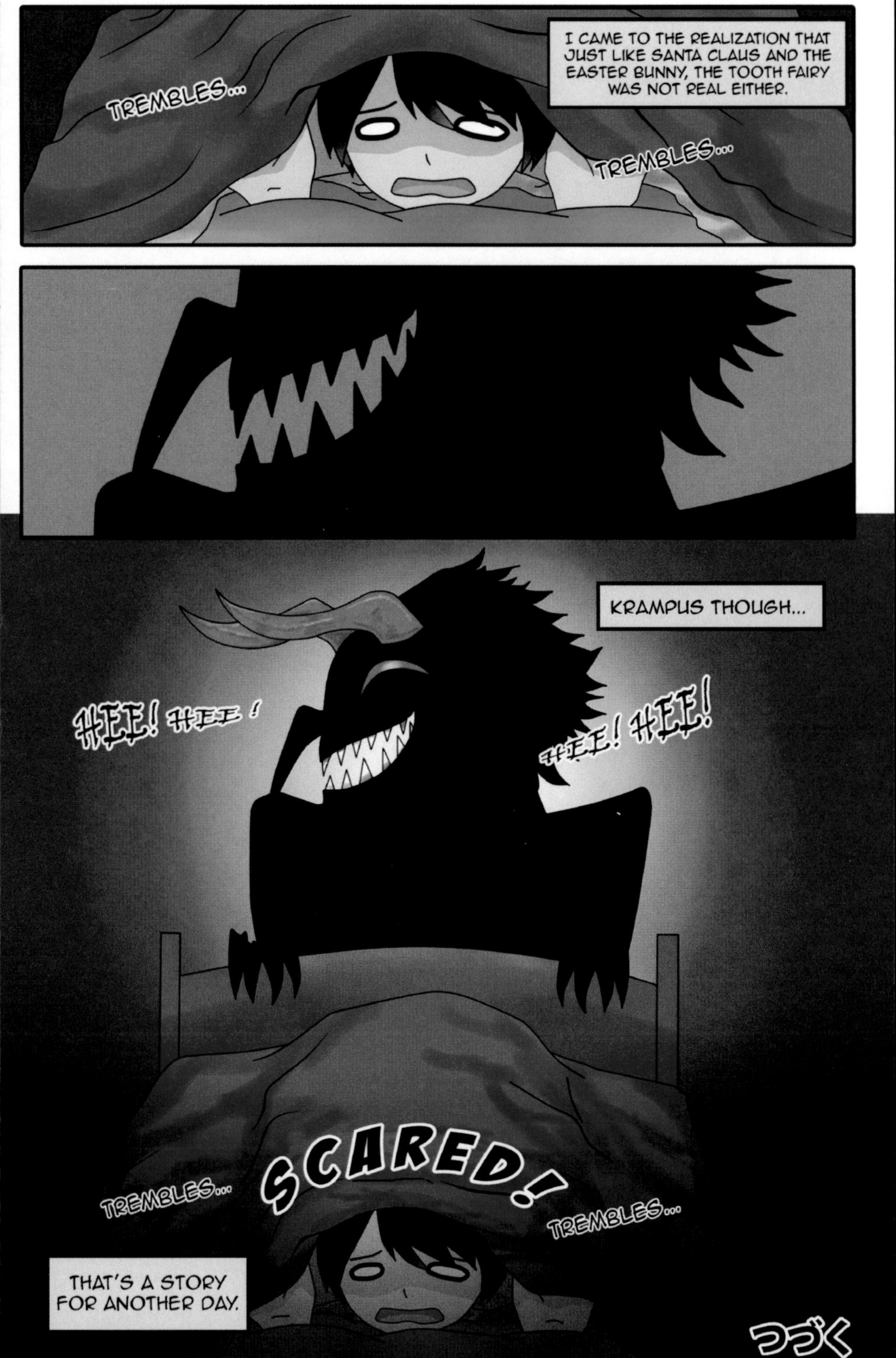
I CAME TO THE REALIZATION THAT JUST LIKE SANTA CLAUS AND THE EASTER BUNNY, THE TOOTH FAIRY WAS NOT REAL EITHER.
TREMBLES...
TREMBLES...
KRAMPUS THOUGH...
HEE! HEE!
HEE! HEE!
SCARED!
TREMBLES...
TREMBLES...
THAT'S A STORY FOR ANOTHER DAY.
つづく

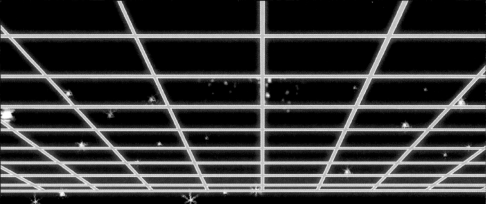

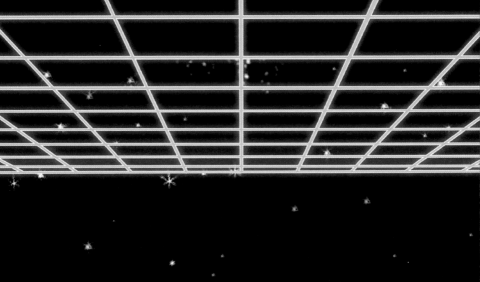

Don't Go in There ...
They'll Kill You!

FOR AS LONG AS I CAN REMEMBER, MOM HAS ALWAYS BEEN OVER-PROTECTIVE OF ME.

WALKS...

WALKS...

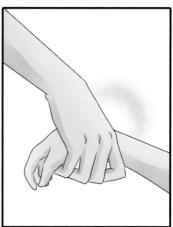

ESPECIALLY WHEN I WAS A KID, MOM WAS CONSTANTLY WORRIED I'D GET LOST, HURT OR WORSE IF I WANDERED OFF ON MY OWN. BEING THE CURIOUS LITTLE "MONKEY" THAT I WAS, I HAD A HABIT OF PULLING DISAPPEARING ACTS ON MOM, VERY MUCH TO HER DISMAY.

RELEASE...

SEARCHES...

WALKS...

OKAY, MONKEY. LET'S GO.

MONKEY! WHERE ARE YOU?

MISSING!

SOMETIMES MOM WAS A LITTLE *TOO* OVERPROTECTIVE AND HAD A TENDENCY TO OVERREACT IN EVEN THE SAFEST OF SITUATIONS.

HALTS!

LOOKS UP...

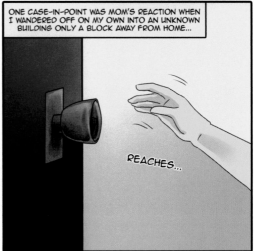

ONE CASE-IN-POINT WAS MOM'S REACTION WHEN I WANDERED OFF ON MY OWN INTO AN UNKNOWN BUILDING ONLY A BLOCK AWAY FROM HOME...

REACHES...

MONKEY!

GASP!

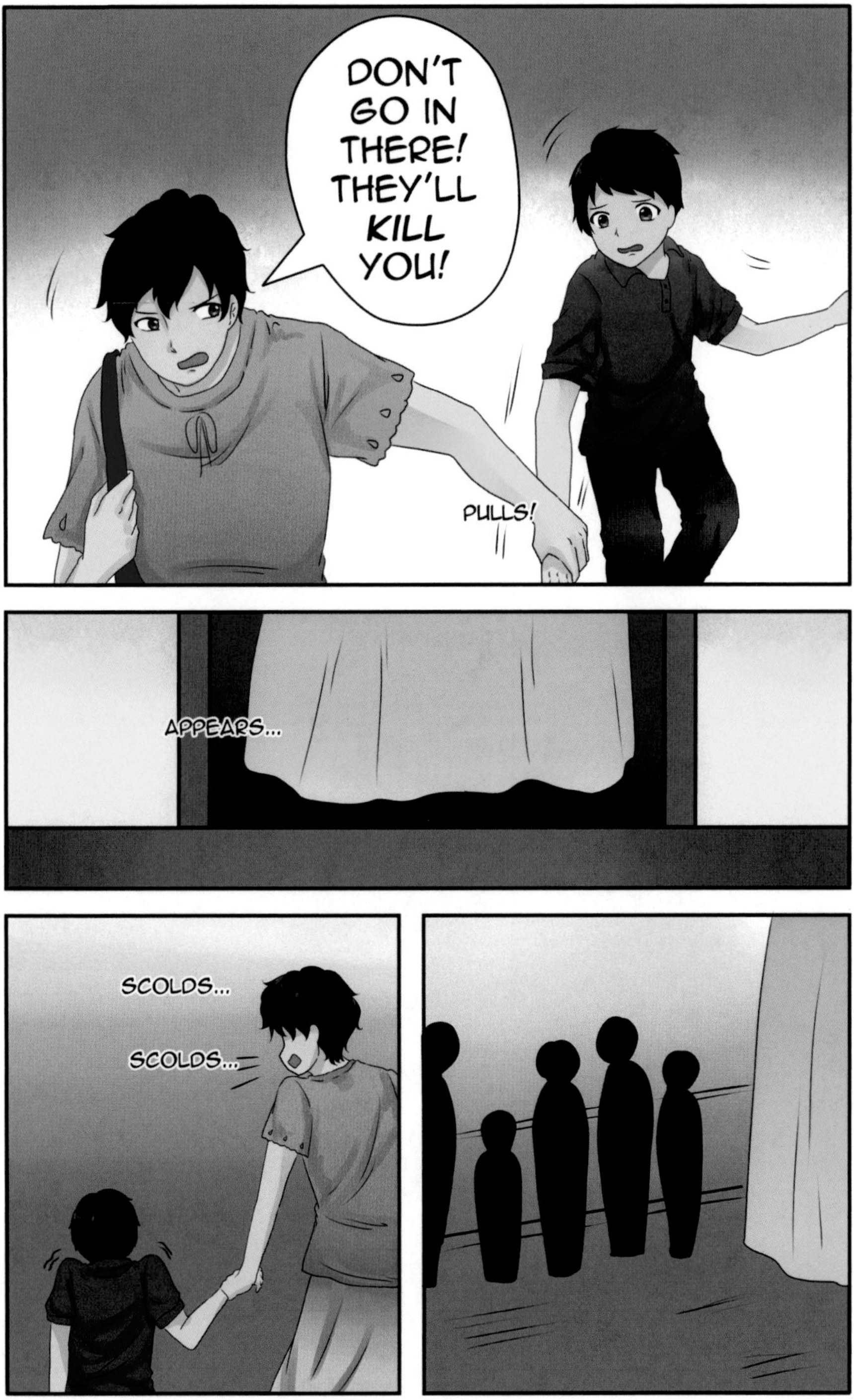
DON'T GO IN THERE! THEY'LL KILL YOU!
PULLS!
APPEARS...
SCOLDS...
SCOLDS...

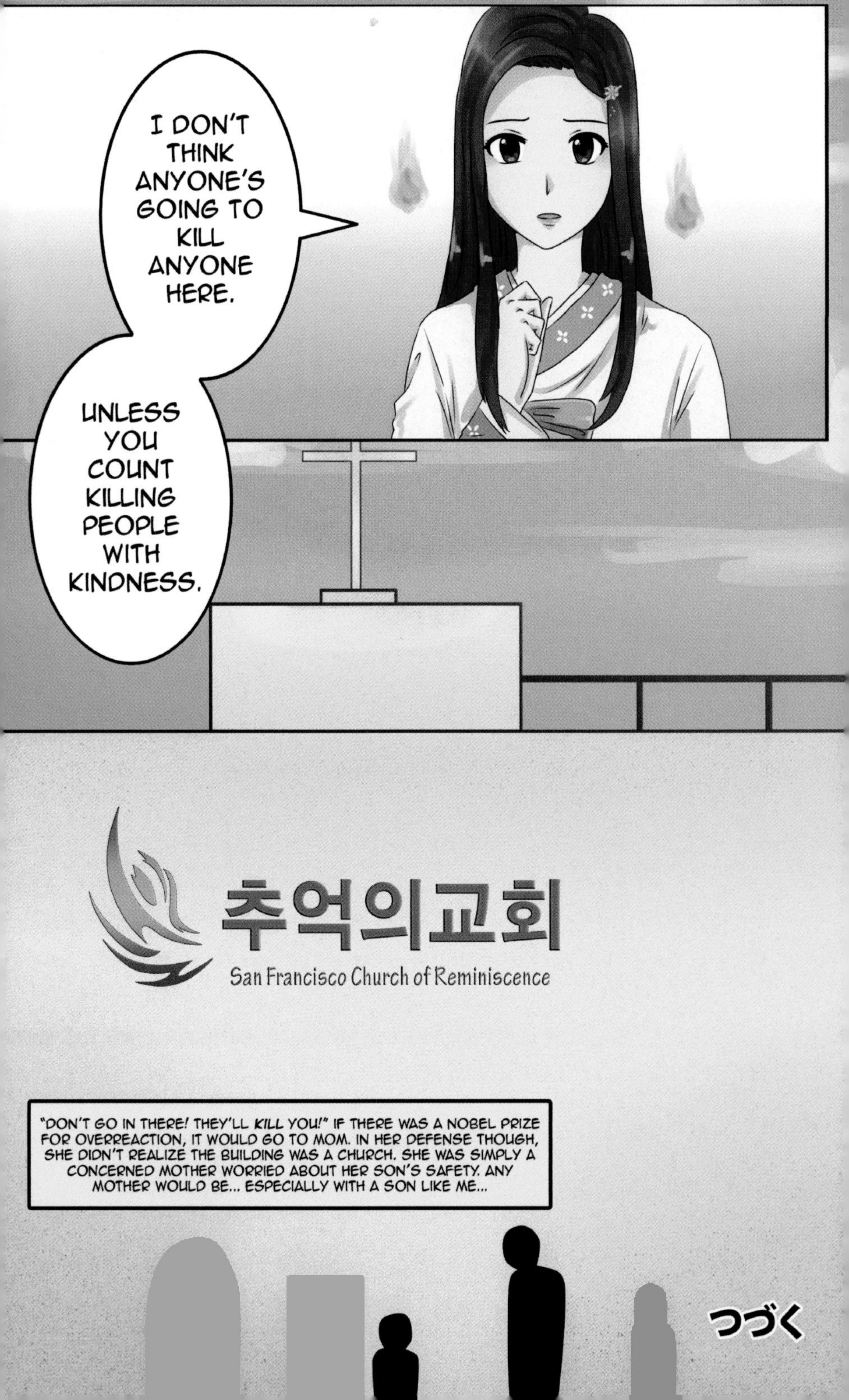
I DON'T THINK ANYONE'S GOING TO KILL ANYONE HERE.
UNLESS YOU COUNT KILLING PEOPLE WITH KINDNESS.
추억의교회
San Francisco Church of Reminiscence
"DON'T GO IN THERE! THEY'LL KILL YOU!" IF THERE WAS A NOBEL PRIZE FOR OVERREACTION, IT WOULD GO TO MOM. IN HER DEFENSE THOUGH, SHE DIDN'T REALIZE THE BUILDING WAS A CHURCH. SHE WAS SIMPLY A CONCERNED MOTHER WORRIED ABOUT HER SON'S SAFETY. ANY MOTHER WOULD BE... ESPECIALLY WITH A SON LIKE ME...
つづく

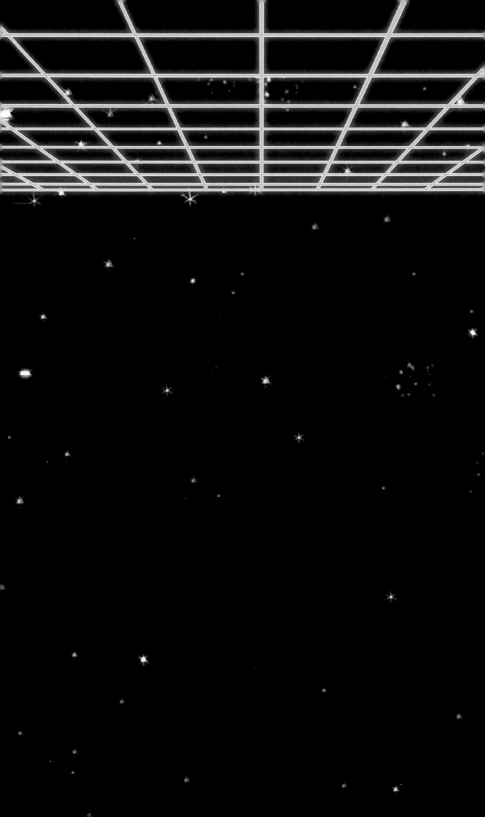

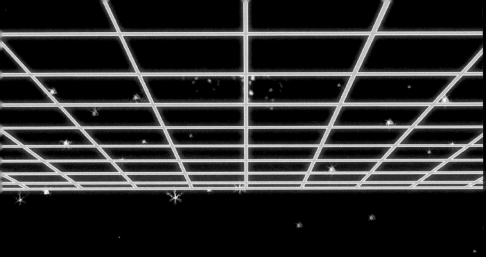

Mom Does What Ninten-don't

WHEN I WAS A KID, I HAD A NINTENDO.

NOT A SUPER NINTENDO.

NOT A NINTENDO 64.

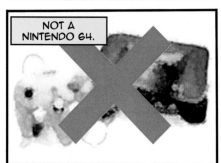

NOT A NINTENDO GAMECUBE.

NOT A NINTENDO WII.

NOT A NINTENDO WII-U.

NOT A NINTENDO SWITCH.

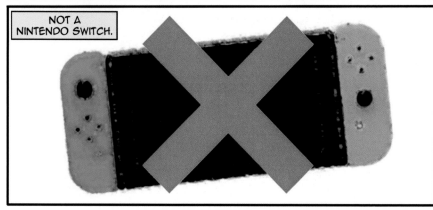

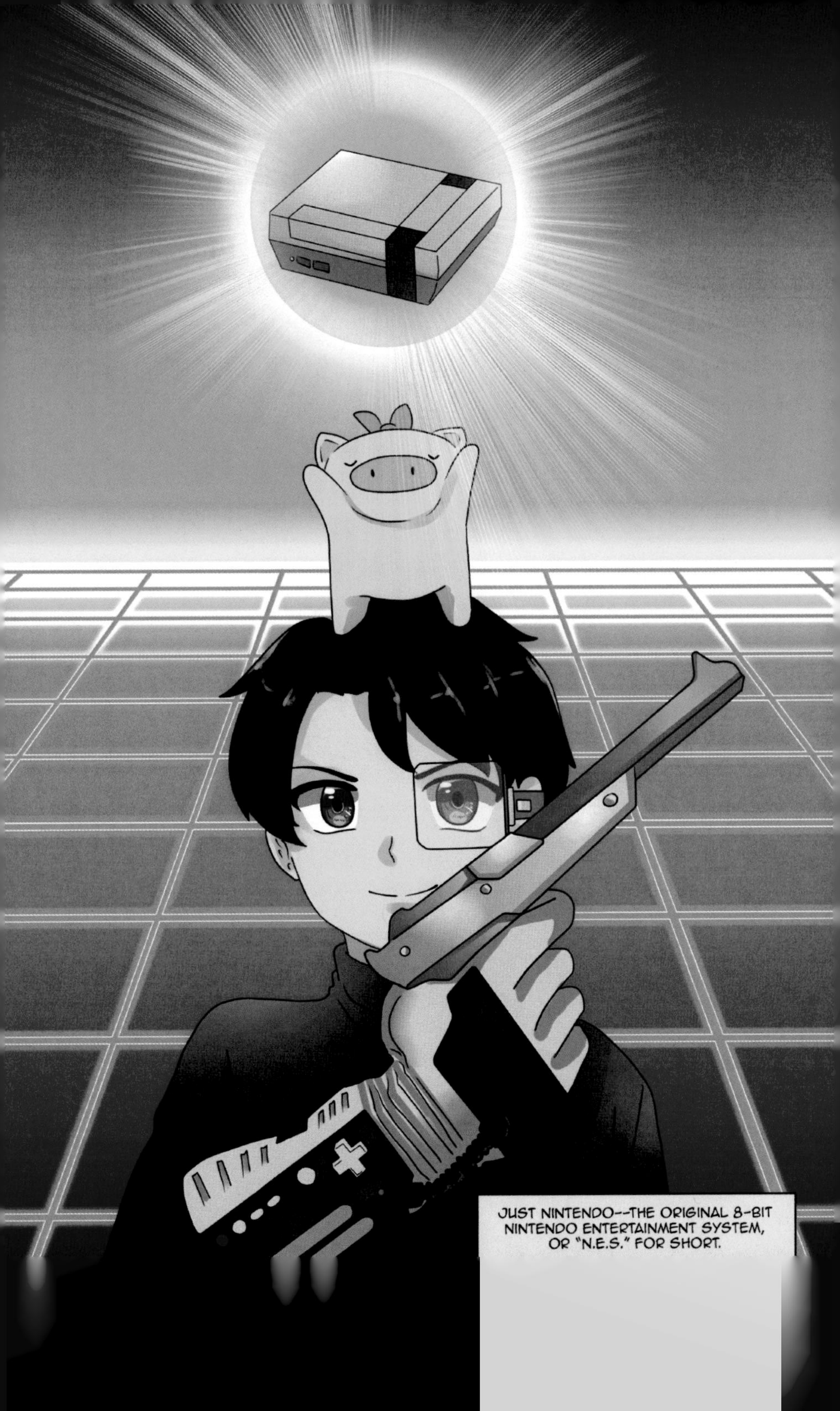
JUST NINTENDO--THE ORIGINAL 8-BIT NINTENDO ENTERTAINMENT SYSTEM, OR "N.E.S." FOR SHORT.

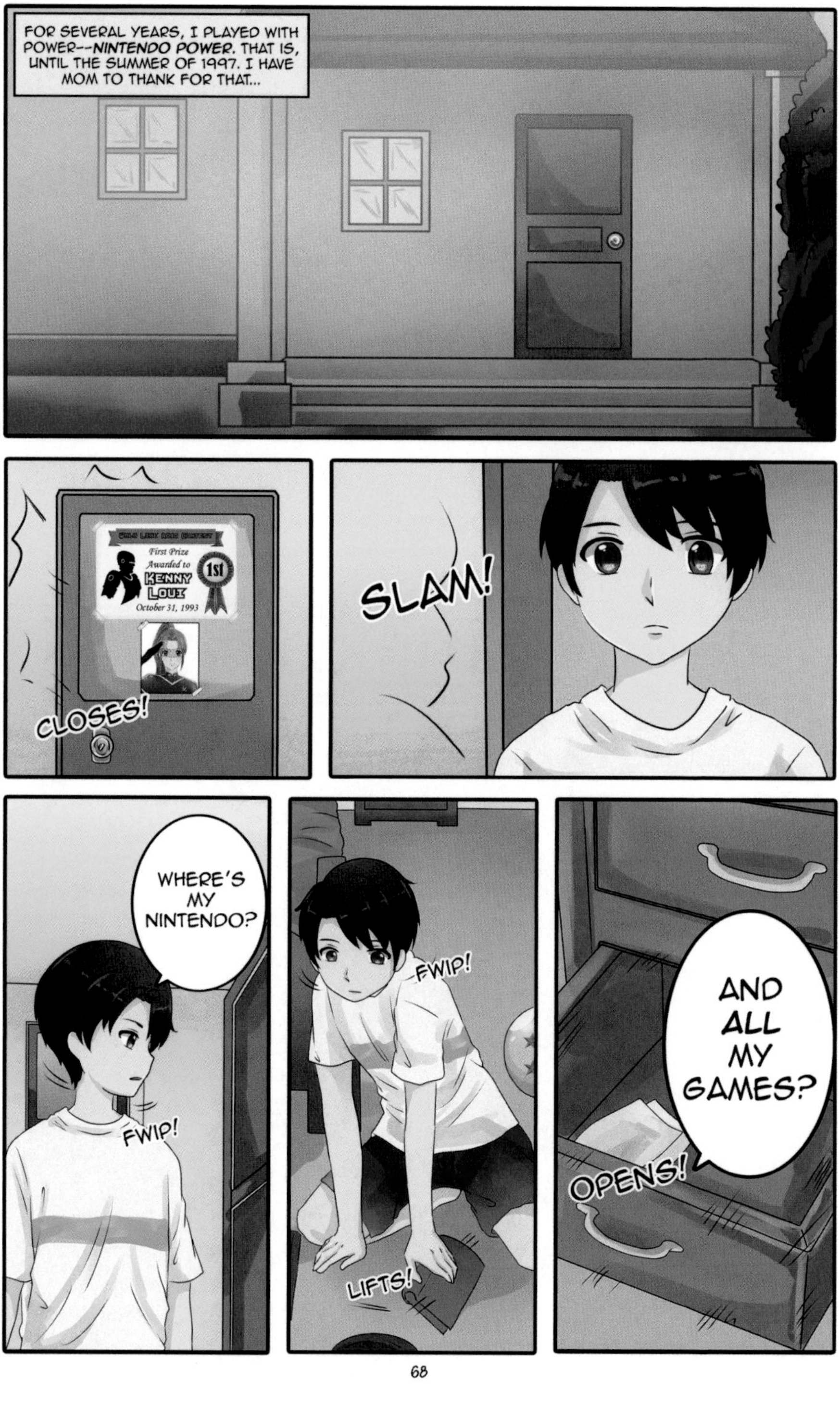
FOR SEVERAL YEARS, I PLAYED WITH POWER--NINTENDO POWER. THAT IS, UNTIL THE SUMMER OF 1997. I HAVE MOM TO THANK FOR THAT...
First Prize
Awarded to
KENNY LOUI
1st
October 31, 1993
CLOSES!
SLAM!
WHERE'S MY NINTENDO?
FWIP!
FWIP!
LIFTS!
AND ALL MY GAMES?
OPENS!

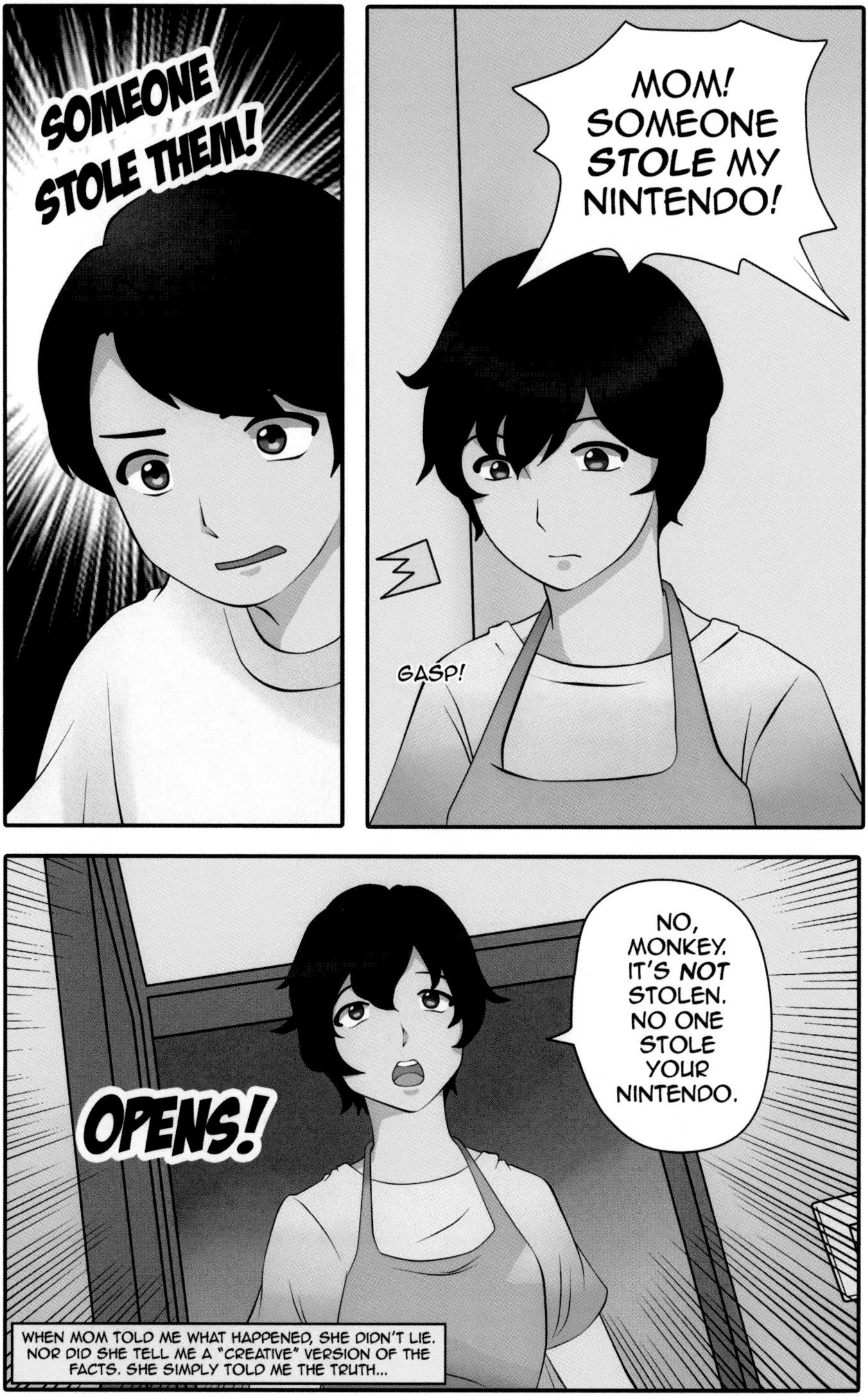
SOMEONE STOLE THEM!
MOM! SOMEONE STOLE MY NINTENDO!
GASP!
OPENS!
NO, MONKEY. IT'S NOT STOLEN. NO ONE STOLE YOUR NINTENDO.
WHEN MOM TOLD ME WHAT HAPPENED, SHE DIDN'T LIE. NOR DID SHE TELL ME A "CREATIVE" VERSION OF THE FACTS. SHE SIMPLY TOLD ME THE TRUTH...

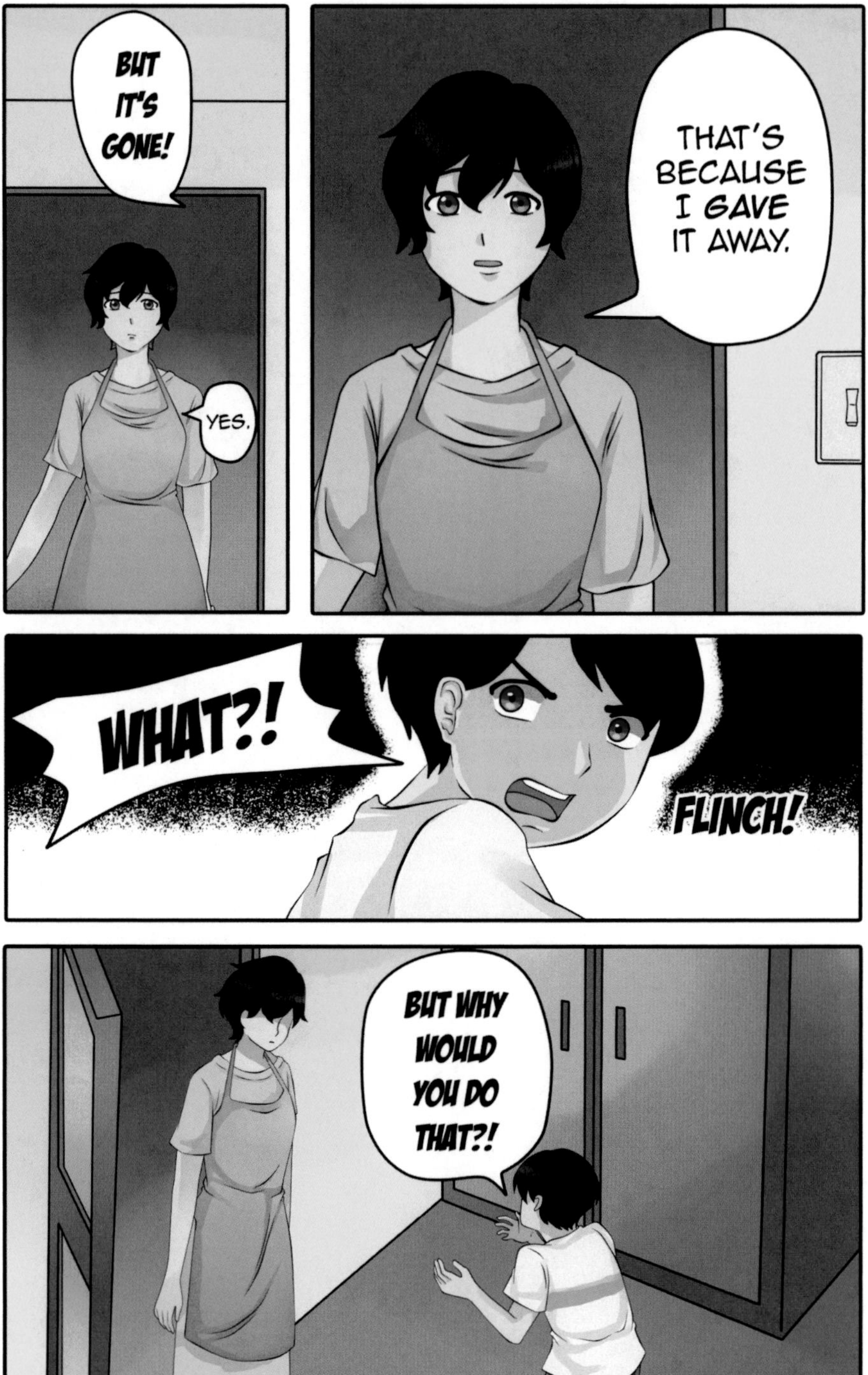
BUT IT'S GONE!
YES.
THAT'S BECAUSE I GAVE IT AWAY.
WHAT?!
FLINCH!
BUT WHY WOULD YOU DO THAT?!

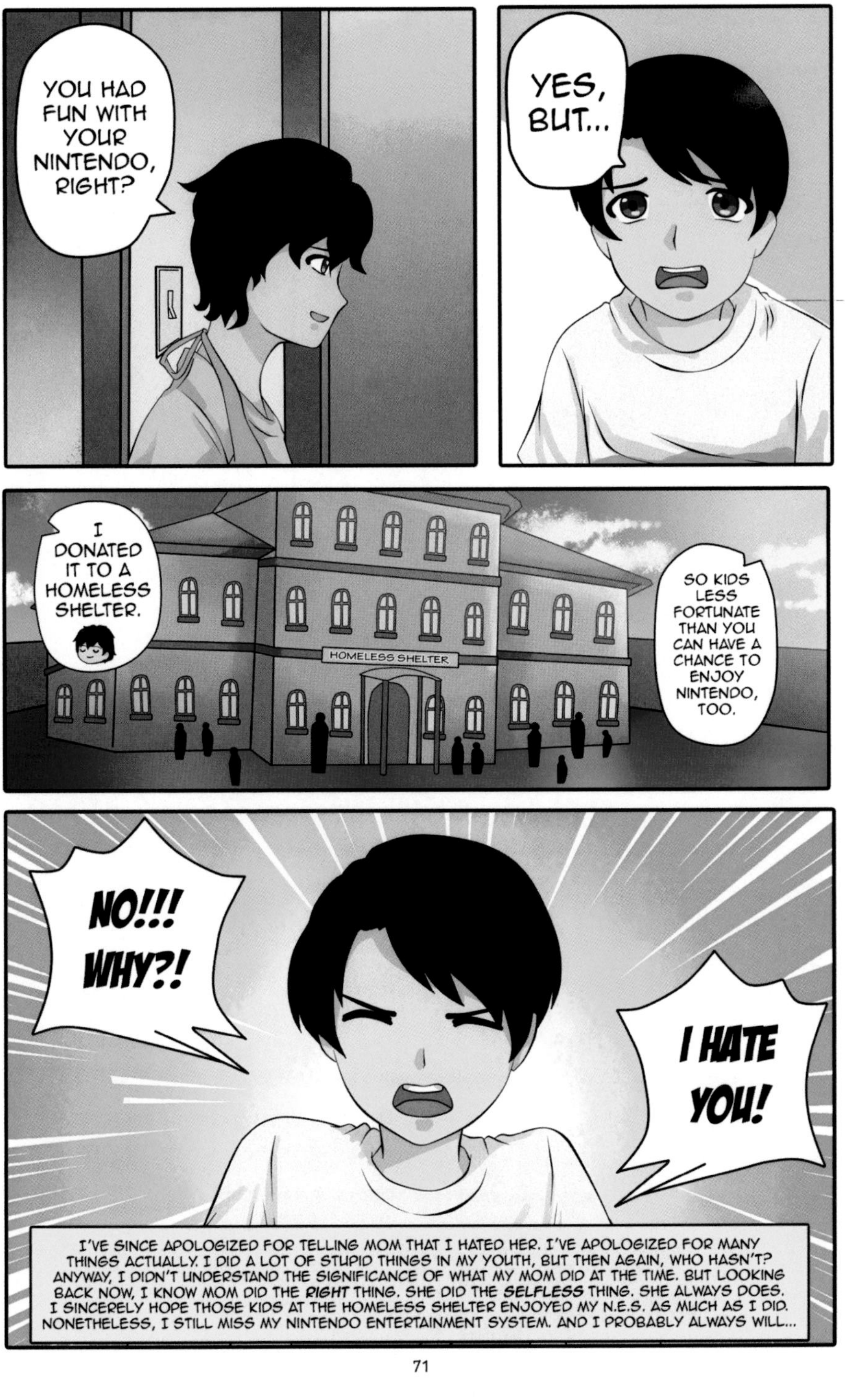
YOU HAD FUN WITH YOUR NINTENDO, RIGHT?
YES, BUT...
I DONATED IT TO A HOMELESS SHELTER.
HOMELESS SHELTER
SO KIDS LESS FORTUNATE THAN YOU CAN HAVE A CHANCE TO ENJOY NINTENDO, TOO.
NO!!! WHY?!
I HATE YOU!
I'VE SINCE APOLOGIZED FOR TELLING MOM THAT I HATED HER. I'VE APOLOGIZED FOR MANY THINGS ACTUALLY. I DID A LOT OF STUPID THINGS IN MY YOUTH, BUT THEN AGAIN, WHO HASN'T? ANYWAY, I DIDN'T UNDERSTAND THE SIGNIFICANCE OF WHAT MY MOM DID AT THE TIME. BUT LOOKING BACK NOW, I KNOW MOM DID THE *RIGHT* THING. SHE DID THE *SELFLESS* THING. SHE ALWAYS DOES. I SINCERELY HOPE THOSE KIDS AT THE HOMELESS SHELTER ENJOYED MY N.E.S. AS MUCH AS I DID. NONETHELESS, I STILL MISS MY NINTENDO ENTERTAINMENT SYSTEM. AND I PROBABLY ALWAYS WILL...

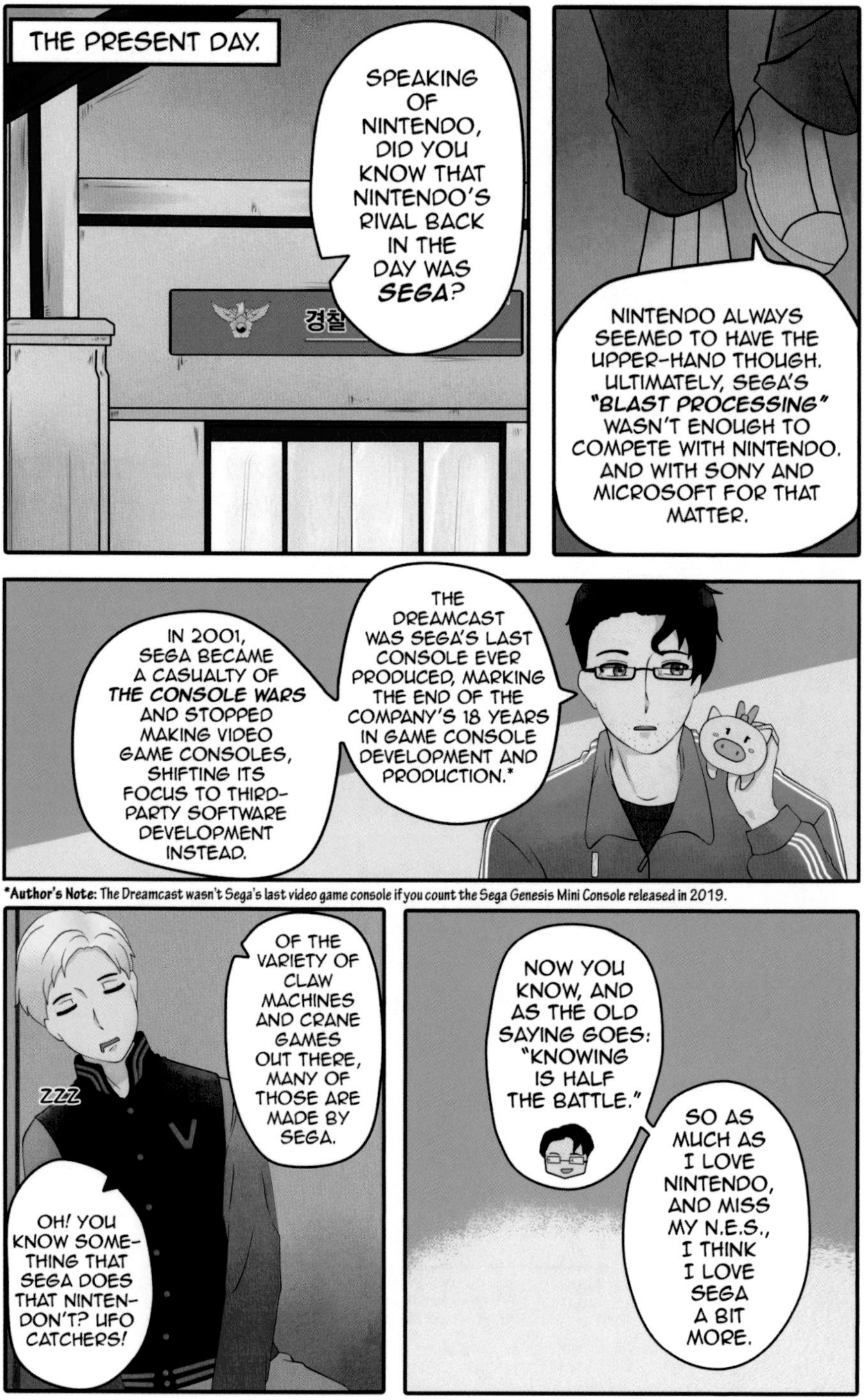
THE PRESENT DAY.
SPEAKING OF NINTENDO, DID YOU KNOW THAT NINTENDO'S RIVAL BACK IN THE DAY WAS SEGA?
경찰
NINTENDO ALWAYS SEEMED TO HAVE THE UPPER-HAND THOUGH. ULTIMATELY, SEGA'S "BLAST PROCESSING" WASN'T ENOUGH TO COMPETE WITH NINTENDO. AND WITH SONY AND MICROSOFT FOR THAT MATTER.
IN 2001, SEGA BECAME A CASUALTY OF THE CONSOLE WARS AND STOPPED MAKING VIDEO GAME CONSOLES, SHIFTING ITS FOCUS TO THIRD-PARTY SOFTWARE DEVELOPMENT INSTEAD.
THE DREAMCAST WAS SEGA'S LAST CONSOLE EVER PRODUCED, MARKING THE END OF THE COMPANY'S 18 YEARS IN GAME CONSOLE DEVELOPMENT AND PRODUCTION.*
OF THE VARIETY OF CLAW MACHINES AND CRANE GAMES OUT THERE, MANY OF THOSE ARE MADE BY SEGA.
ZZZ
OH! YOU KNOW SOME-THING THAT SEGA DOES THAT NINTEN-DON'T? UFO CATCHERS!
NOW YOU KNOW, AND AS THE OLD SAYING GOES: "KNOWING IS HALF THE BATTLE."
SO AS MUCH AS I LOVE NINTENDO, AND MISS MY N.E.S., I THINK I LOVE SEGA A BIT MORE.

***Author's Note:** The Dreamcast wasn't Sega's last video game console if you count the Sega Genesis Mini Console released in 2019.

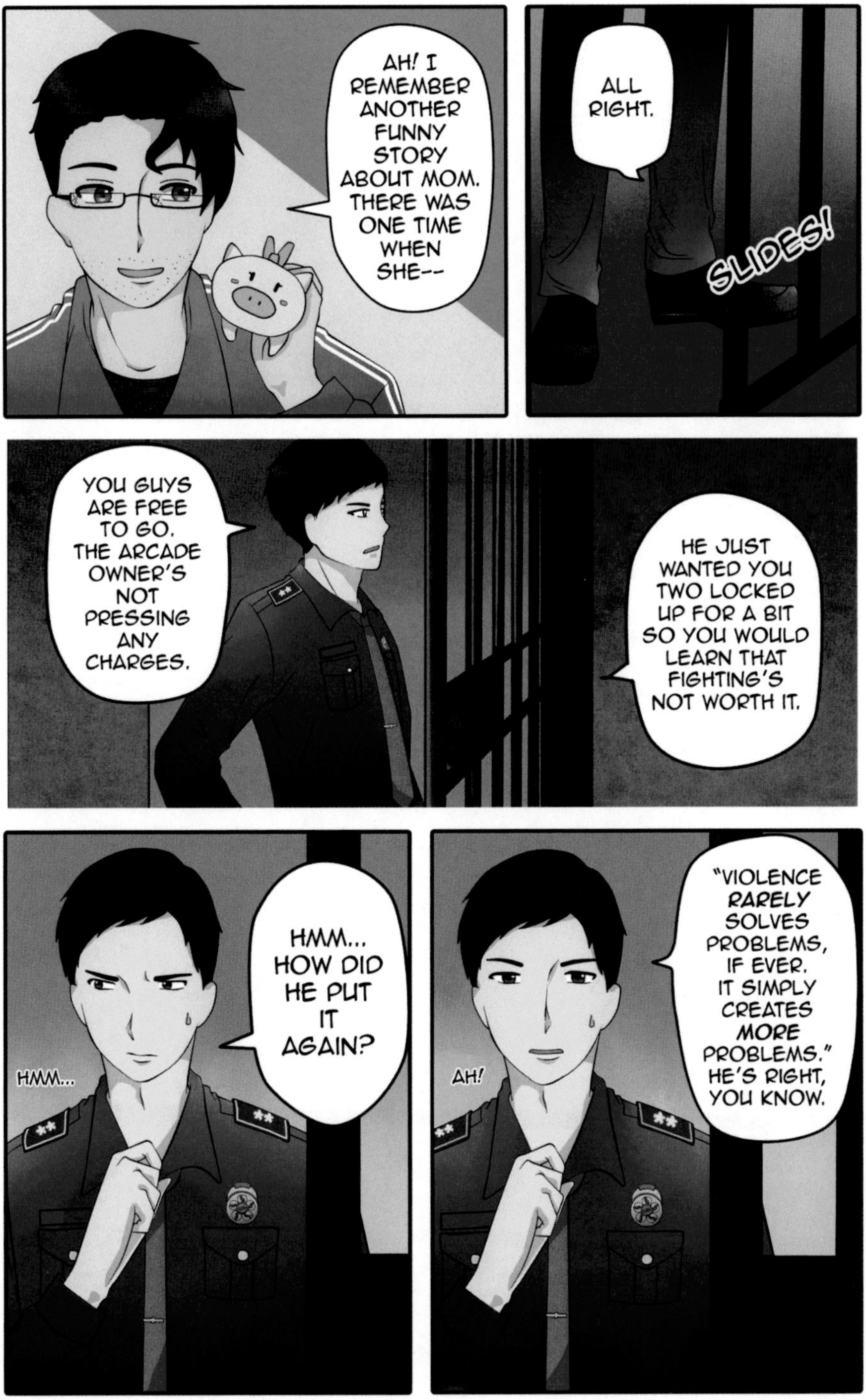
AH! I REMEMBER ANOTHER FUNNY STORY ABOUT MOM. THERE WAS ONE TIME WHEN SHE--
ALL RIGHT.
SLIDES!
YOU GUYS ARE FREE TO GO. THE ARCADE OWNER'S NOT PRESSING ANY CHARGES.
HE JUST WANTED YOU TWO LOCKED UP FOR A BIT SO YOU WOULD LEARN THAT FIGHTING'S NOT WORTH IT.
HMM...
HMM... HOW DID HE PUT IT AGAIN?
AH!
"VIOLENCE RARELY SOLVES PROBLEMS, IF EVER. IT SIMPLY CREATES MORE PROBLEMS." HE'S RIGHT, YOU KNOW.

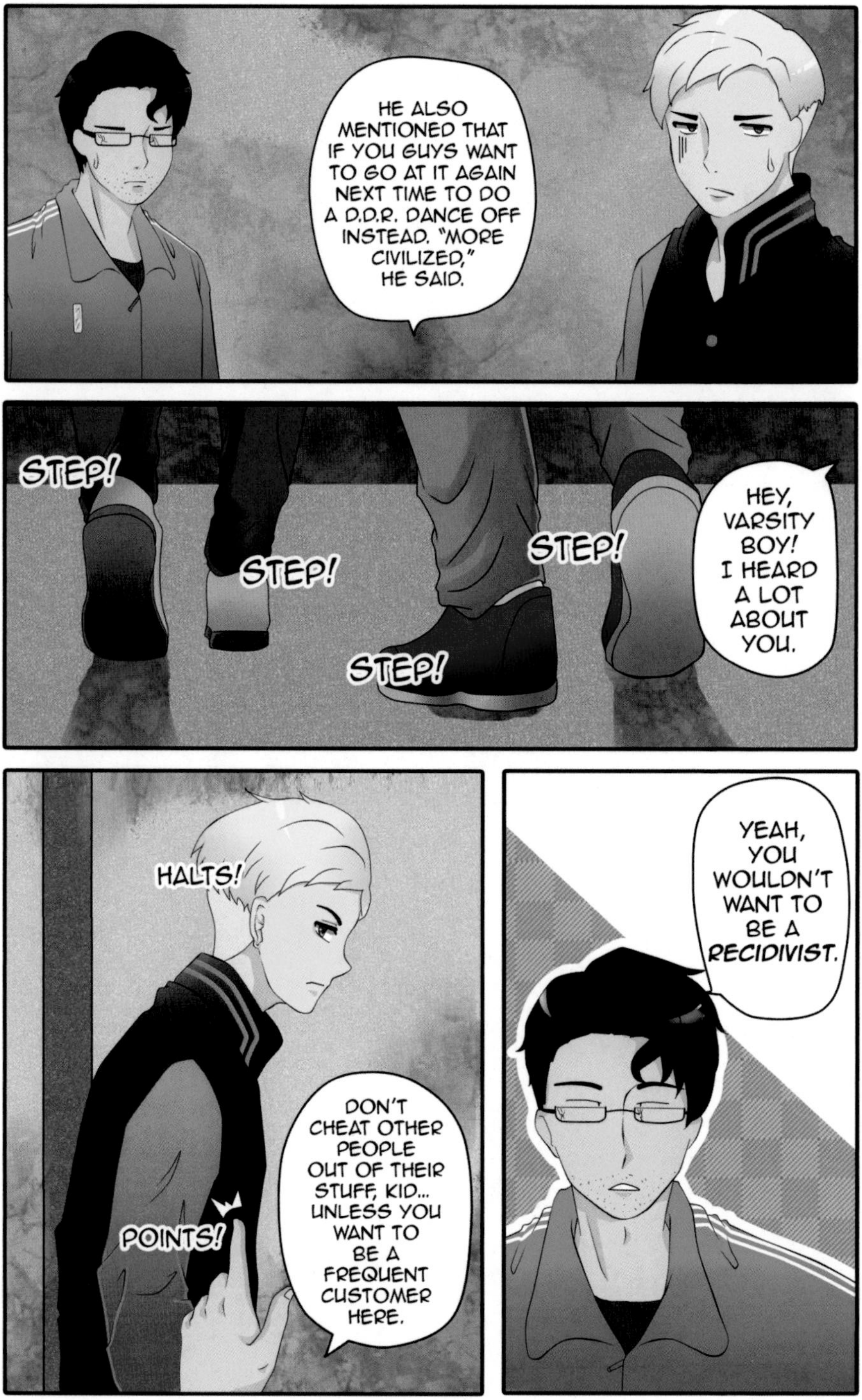
HE ALSO MENTIONED THAT IF YOU GUYS WANT TO GO AT IT AGAIN NEXT TIME TO DO A D.D.R. DANCE OFF INSTEAD. "MORE CIVILIZED," HE SAID.
STEP!
STEP!
STEP!
STEP!
HEY, VARSITY BOY! I HEARD A LOT ABOUT YOU.
HALTS!
POINTS!
DON'T CHEAT OTHER PEOPLE OUT OF THEIR STUFF, KID... UNLESS YOU WANT TO BE A FREQUENT CUSTOMER HERE.
YEAH, YOU WOULDN'T WANT TO BE A *RECIDIVIST*.

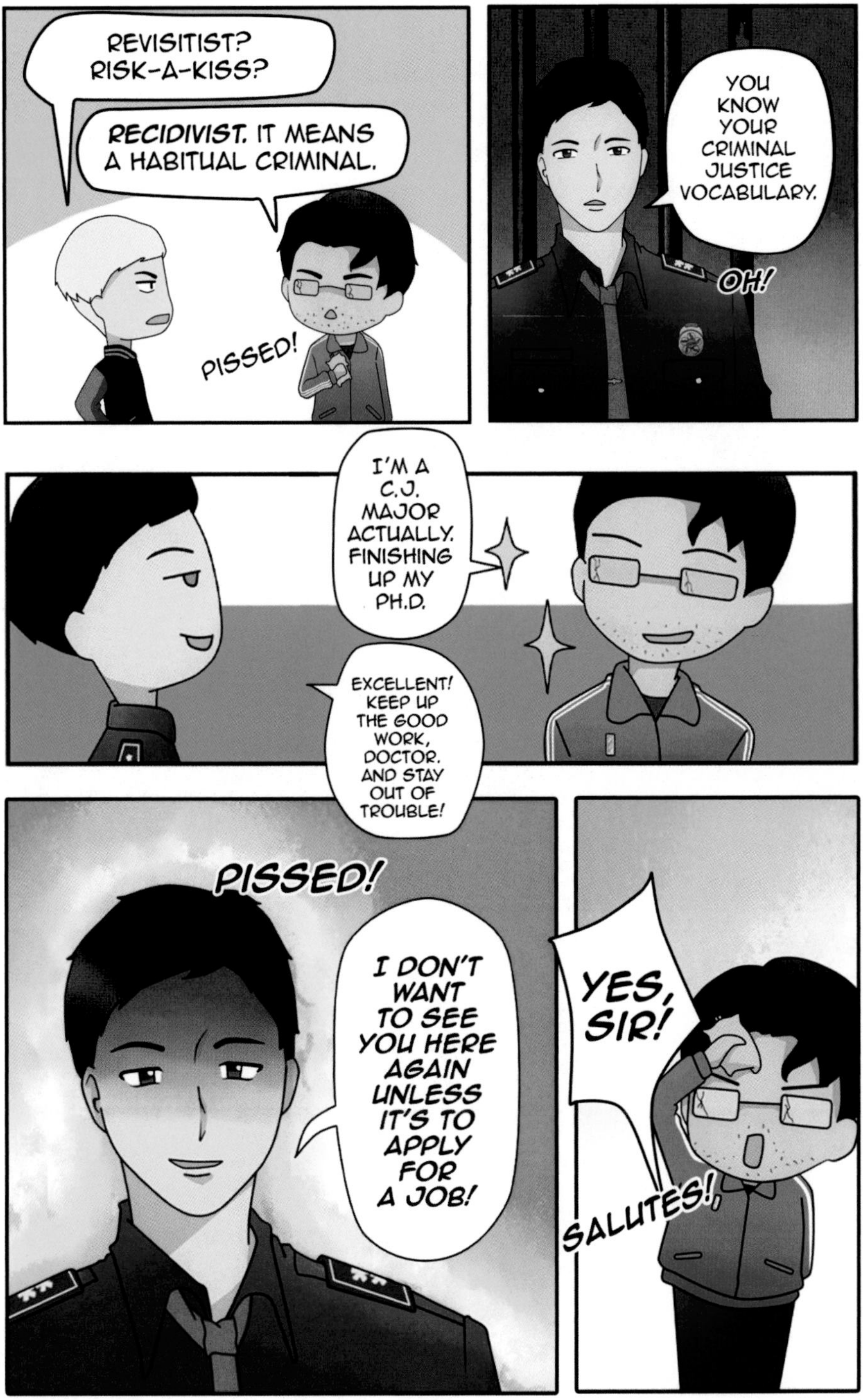
REVISITIST? RISK-A-KISS?
RECIDIVIST. IT MEANS A HABITUAL CRIMINAL.
PISSED!
YOU KNOW YOUR CRIMINAL JUSTICE VOCABULARY.
OH!
I'M A C.J. MAJOR ACTUALLY. FINISHING UP MY PH.D.
EXCELLENT! KEEP UP THE GOOD WORK, DOCTOR. AND STAY OUT OF TROUBLE!
PISSED!
I DON'T WANT TO SEE YOU HERE AGAIN UNLESS IT'S TO APPLY FOR A JOB!
YES, SIR!
SALUTES!

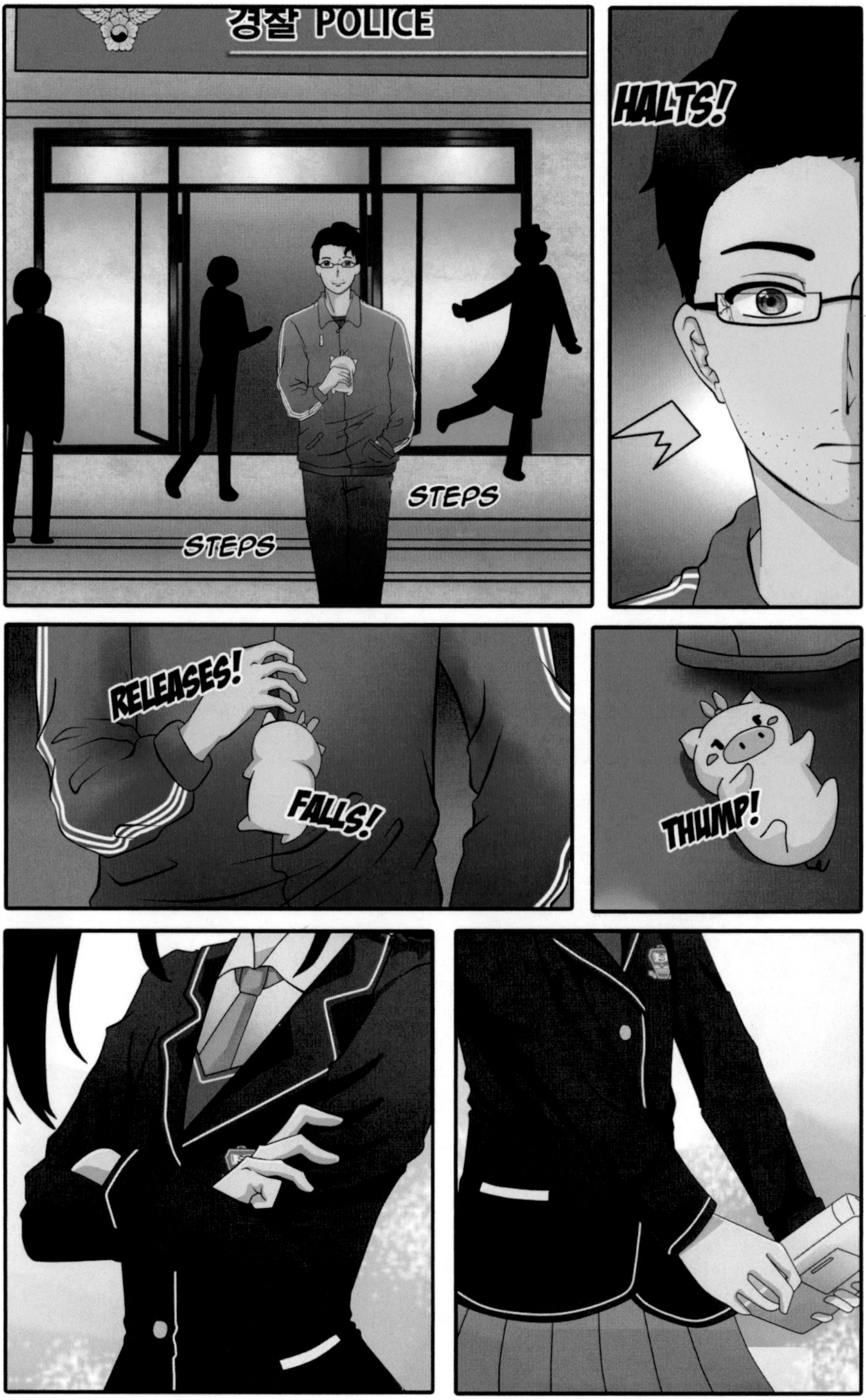
경찰 POLICE
STEPS
STEPS
HALTS!
RELEASES!
FALLS!
THUMP!

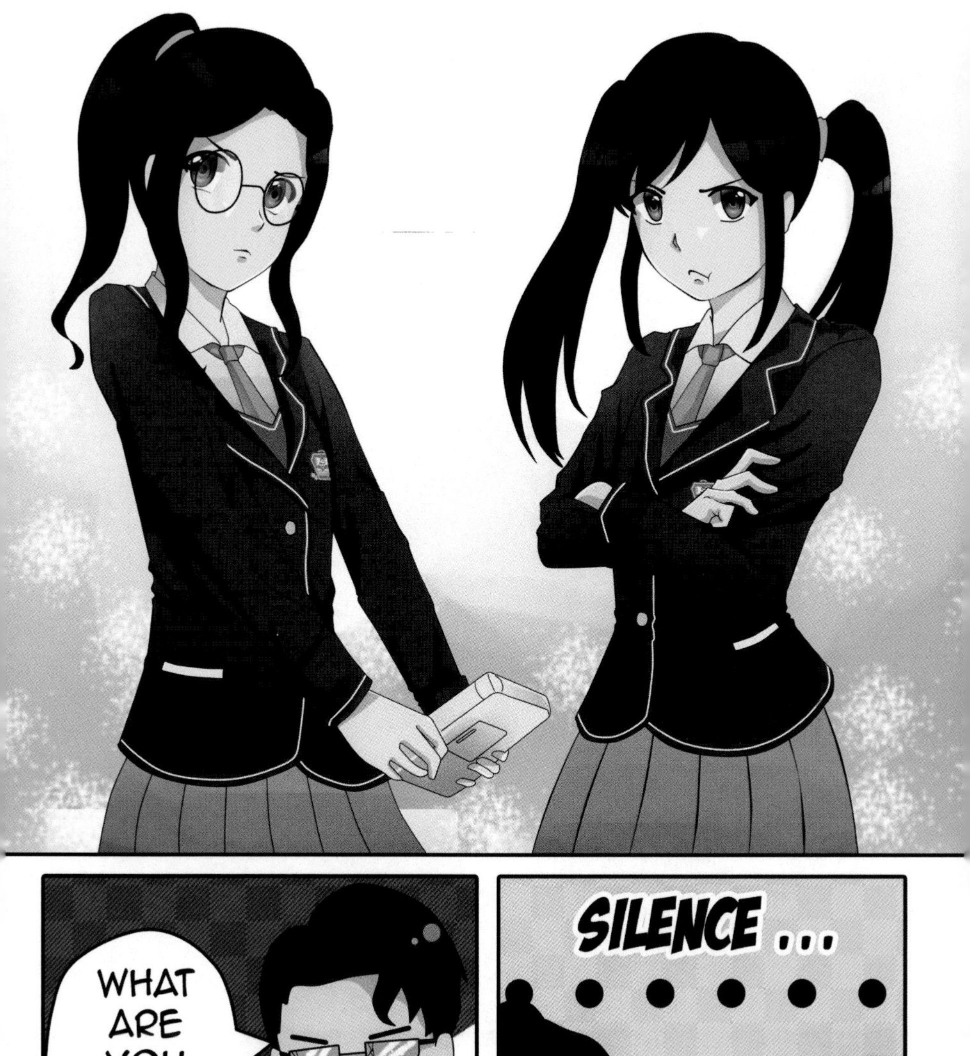

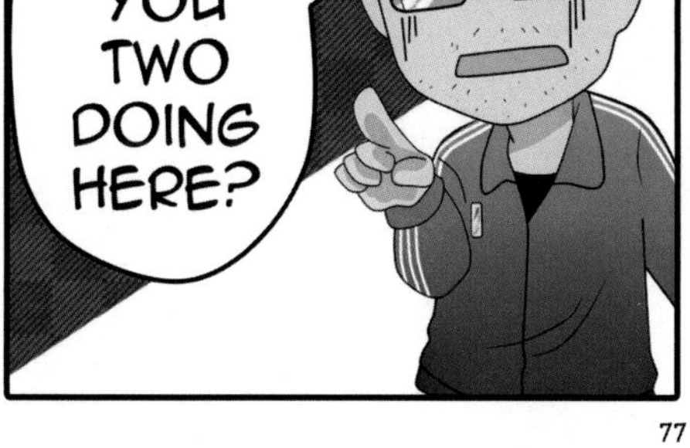
WHAT ARE YOU TWO DOING HERE?

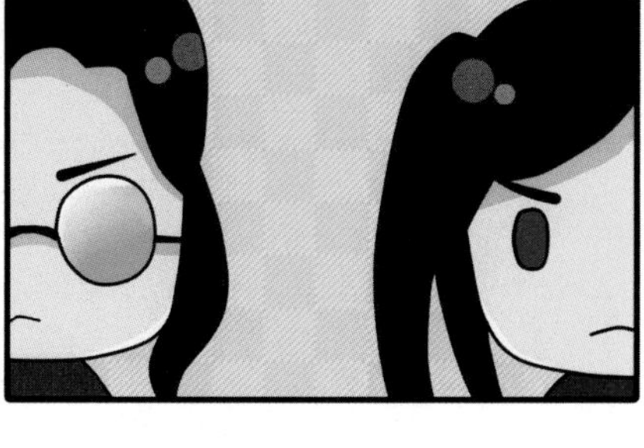
SILENCE ...

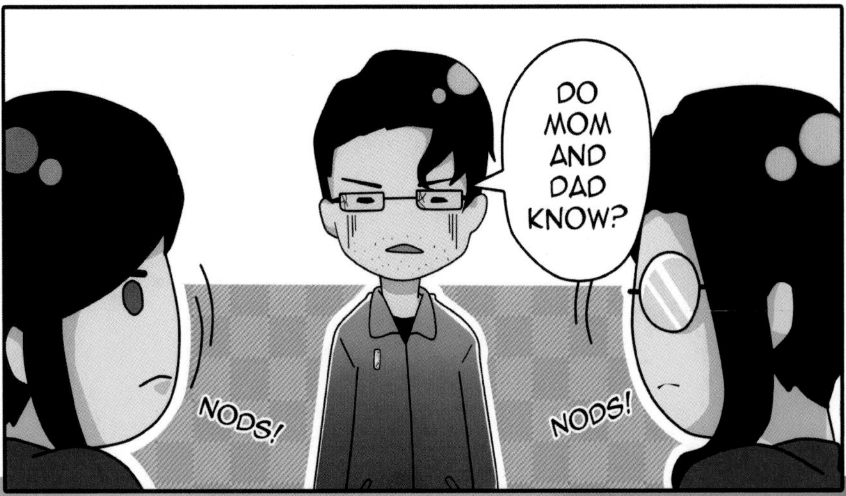
DO MOM AND DAD KNOW?
NODS!
NODS!

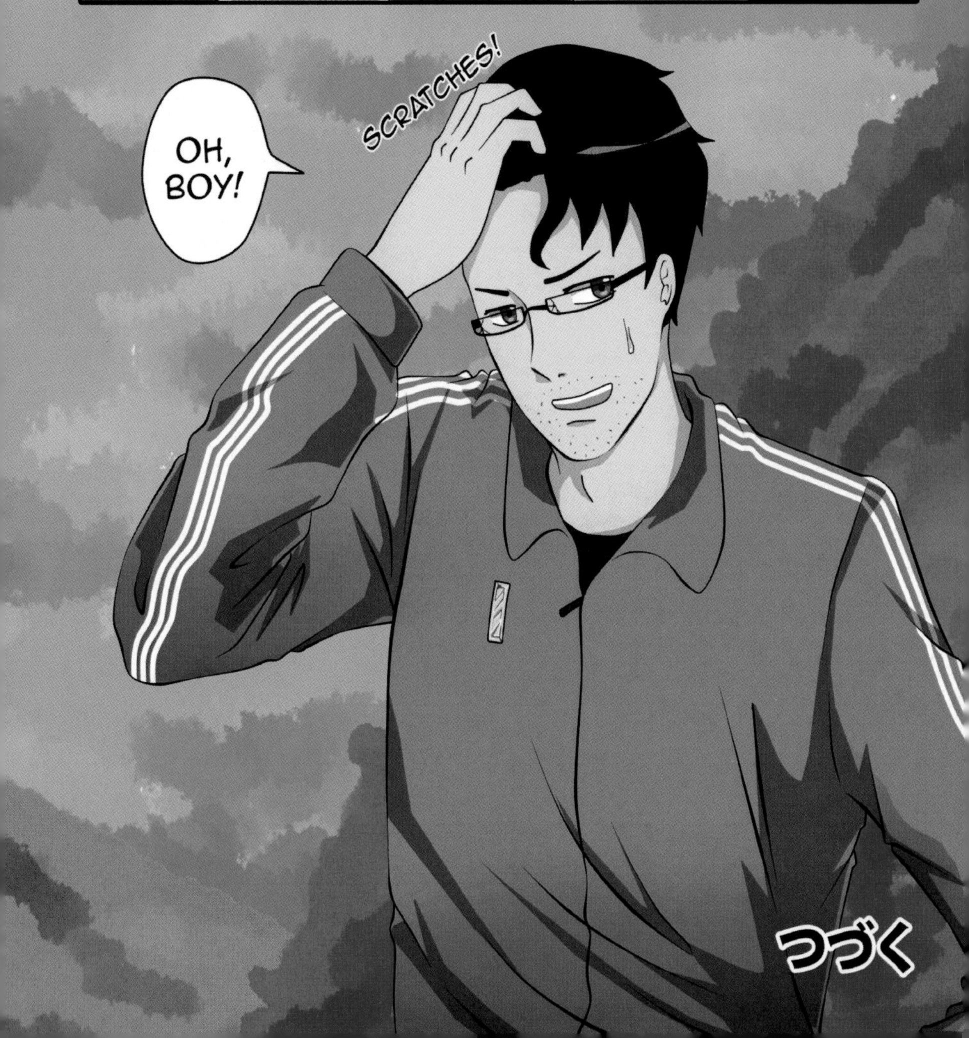
SCRATCHES!
OH, BOY!
つづく

Bonus Story:
The Lie I Told My Mother

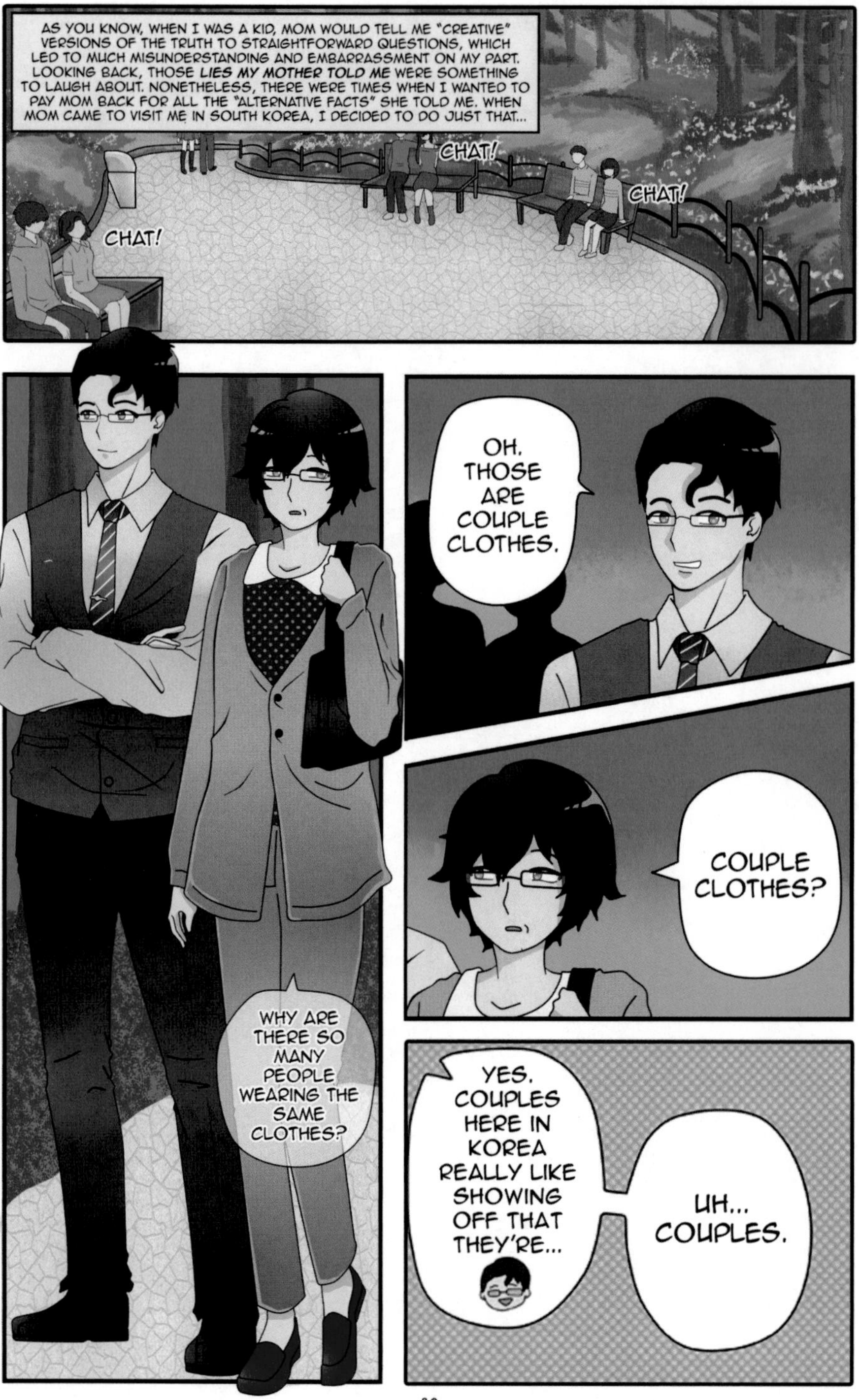
AS YOU KNOW, WHEN I WAS A KID, MOM WOULD TELL ME "CREATIVE" VERSIONS OF THE TRUTH TO STRAIGHTFORWARD QUESTIONS, WHICH LED TO MUCH MISUNDERSTANDING AND EMBARRASSMENT ON MY PART. LOOKING BACK, THOSE *LIES MY MOTHER TOLD ME* WERE SOMETHING TO LAUGH ABOUT. NONETHELESS, THERE WERE TIMES WHEN I WANTED TO PAY MOM BACK FOR ALL THE "ALTERNATIVE FACTS" SHE TOLD ME. WHEN MOM CAME TO VISIT ME IN SOUTH KOREA, I DECIDED TO DO JUST THAT...
CHAT!
CHAT!
CHAT!
WHY ARE THERE SO MANY PEOPLE WEARING THE SAME CLOTHES?
OH. THOSE ARE COUPLE CLOTHES.
COUPLE CLOTHES?
YES. COUPLES HERE IN KOREA REALLY LIKE SHOWING OFF THAT THEY'RE...
UH... COUPLES.

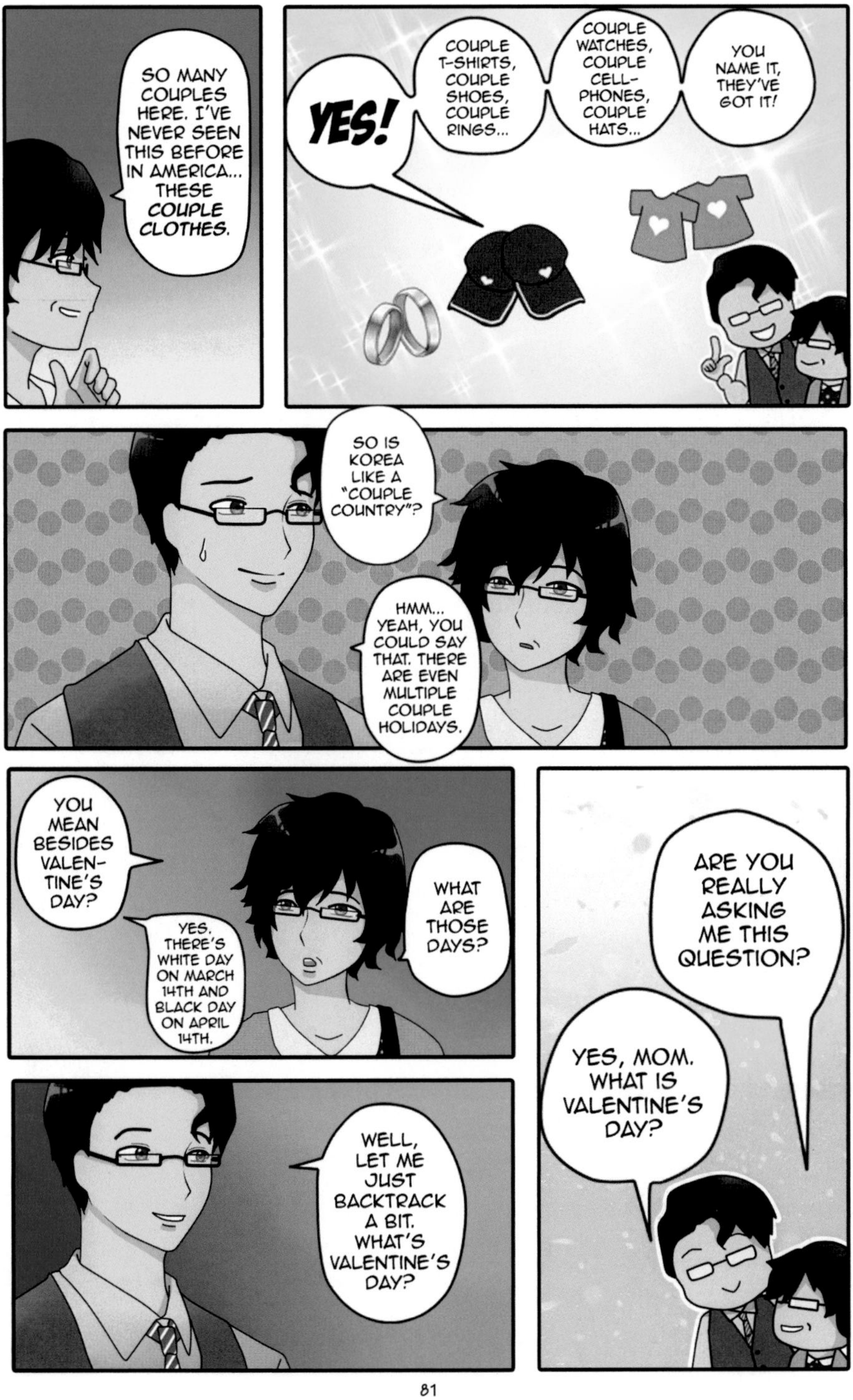
SO MANY COUPLES HERE. I'VE NEVER SEEN THIS BEFORE IN AMERICA... THESE COUPLE CLOTHES.
YES!
COUPLE T-SHIRTS, COUPLE SHOES, COUPLE RINGS...
COUPLE WATCHES, COUPLE CELL-PHONES, COUPLE HATS...
YOU NAME IT, THEY'VE GOT IT!
SO IS KOREA LIKE A "COUPLE COUNTRY"?
HMM... YEAH, YOU COULD SAY THAT. THERE ARE EVEN MULTIPLE COUPLE HOLIDAYS.
YOU MEAN BESIDES VALEN-TINE'S DAY?
YES. THERE'S WHITE DAY ON MARCH 14TH AND BLACK DAY ON APRIL 14TH.
WHAT ARE THOSE DAYS?
WELL, LET ME JUST BACKTRACK A BIT. WHAT'S VALENTINE'S DAY?
ARE YOU REALLY ASKING ME THIS QUESTION?
YES, MOM. WHAT IS VALENTINE'S DAY?

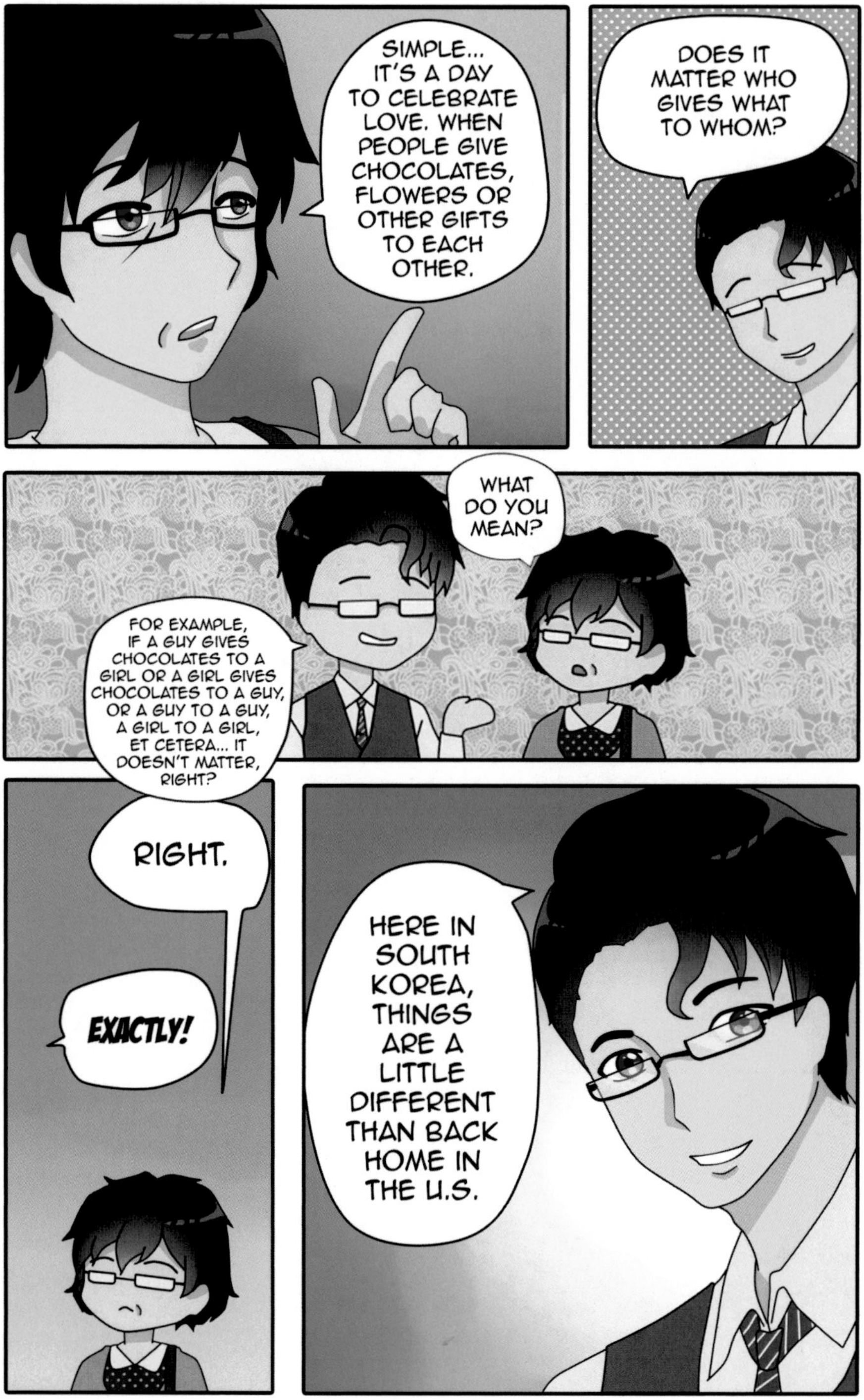
SIMPLE... IT'S A DAY TO CELEBRATE LOVE. WHEN PEOPLE GIVE CHOCOLATES, FLOWERS OR OTHER GIFTS TO EACH OTHER.
DOES IT MATTER WHO GIVES WHAT TO WHOM?
WHAT DO YOU MEAN?
FOR EXAMPLE, IF A GUY GIVES CHOCOLATES TO A GIRL OR A GIRL GIVES CHOCOLATES TO A GUY, OR A GUY TO A GUY, A GIRL TO A GIRL, ET CETERA... IT DOESN'T MATTER, RIGHT?
RIGHT.
EXACTLY!
HERE IN SOUTH KOREA, THINGS ARE A LITTLE DIFFERENT THAN BACK HOME IN THE U.S.

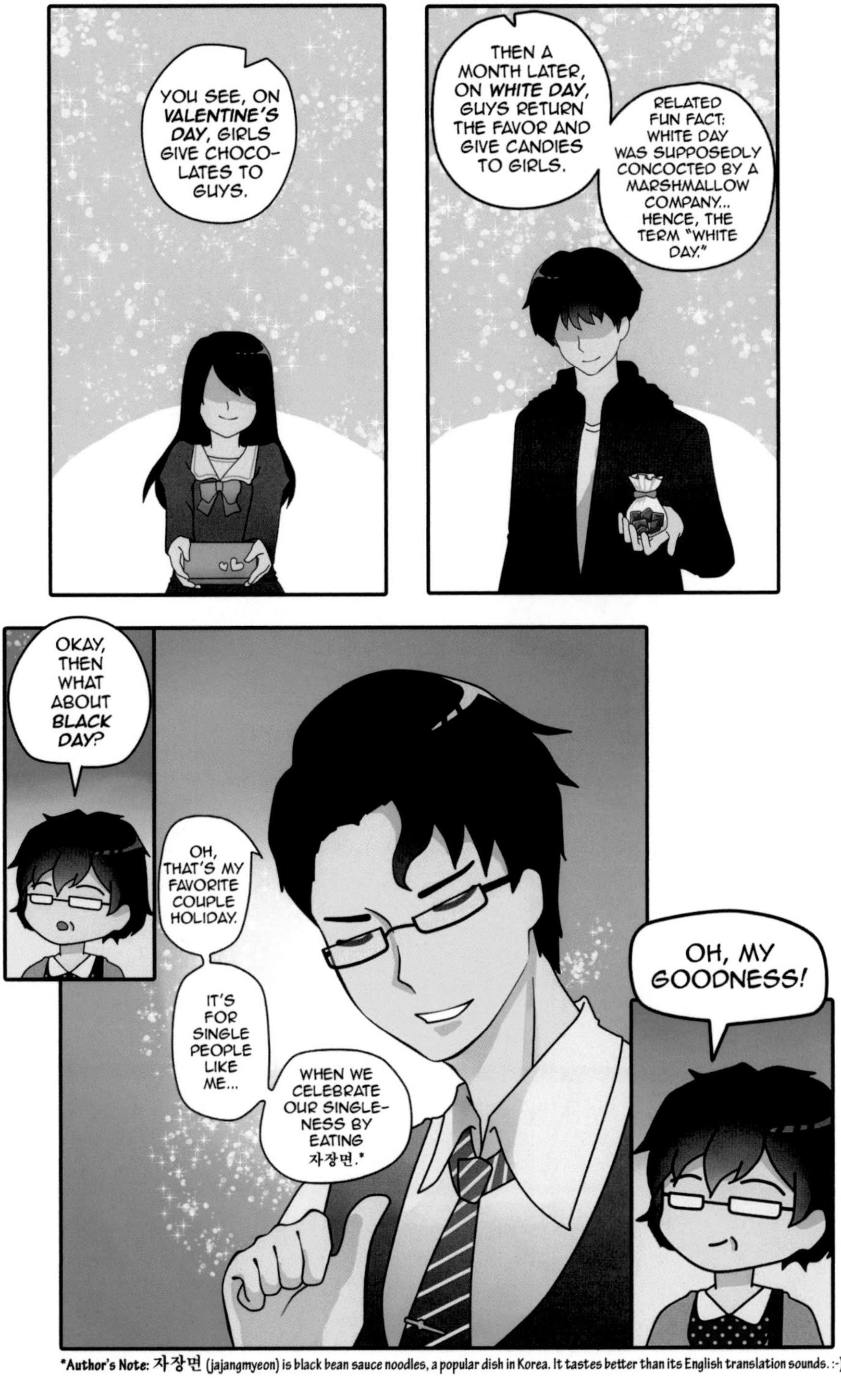
YOU SEE, ON VALENTINE'S DAY, GIRLS GIVE CHOCO-LATES TO GUYS.
THEN A MONTH LATER, ON WHITE DAY, GUYS RETURN THE FAVOR AND GIVE CANDIES TO GIRLS.
RELATED FUN FACT: WHITE DAY WAS SUPPOSEDLY CONCOCTED BY A MARSHMALLOW COMPANY... HENCE, THE TERM "WHITE DAY."
OKAY, THEN WHAT ABOUT BLACK DAY?
OH, THAT'S MY FAVORITE COUPLE HOLIDAY.
IT'S FOR SINGLE PEOPLE LIKE ME...
WHEN WE CELEBRATE OUR SINGLE-NESS BY EATING 자장면.*
OH, MY GOODNESS!

*Author's Note: 자장면 (jajangmyeon) is black bean sauce noodles, a popular dish in Korea. It tastes better than its English translation sounds. :-)

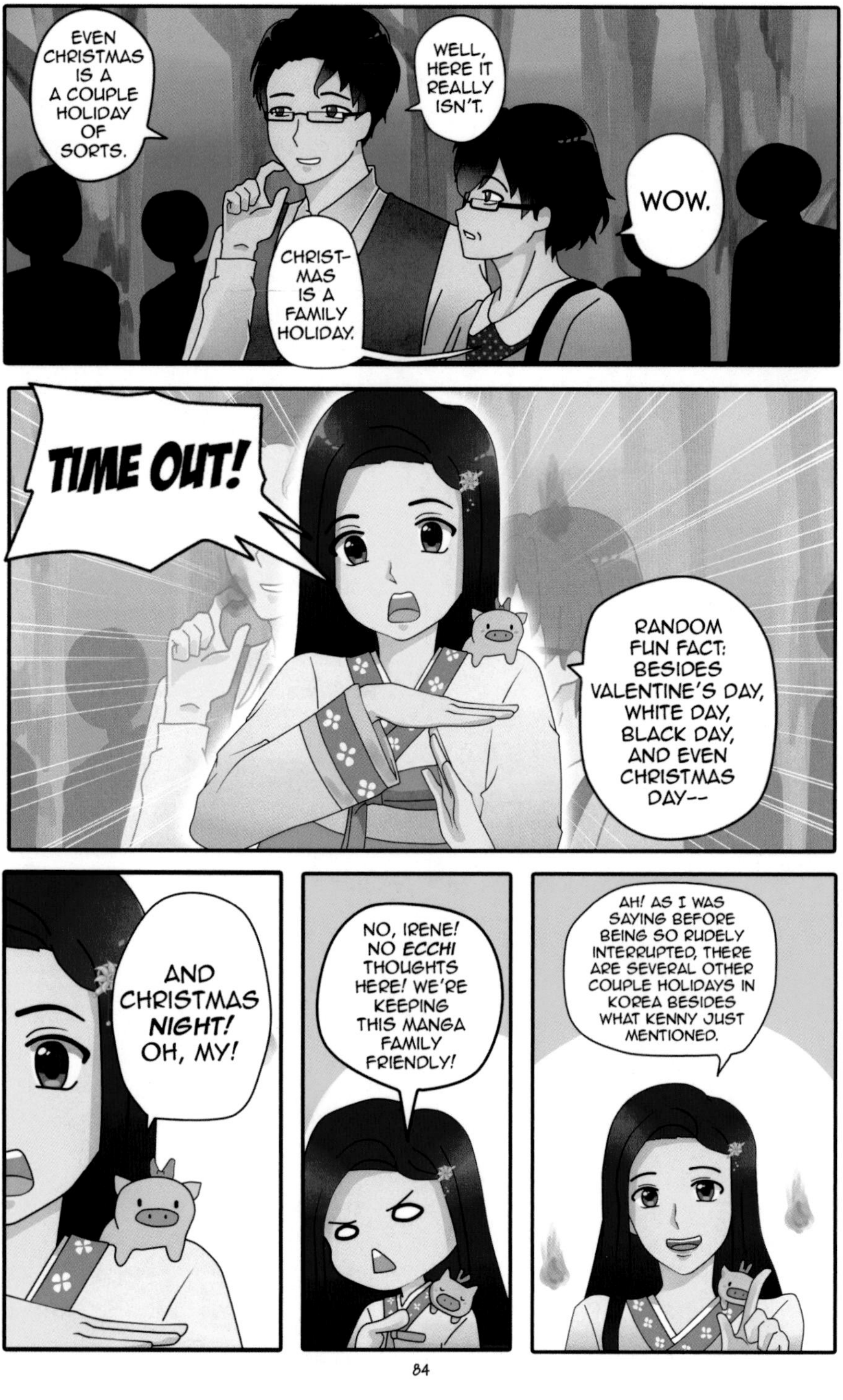
EVEN CHRISTMAS IS A A COUPLE HOLIDAY OF SORTS.
WELL, HERE IT REALLY ISN'T.
CHRIST-MAS IS A FAMILY HOLIDAY.
WOW.
TIME OUT!
RANDOM FUN FACT: BESIDES VALENTINE'S DAY, WHITE DAY, BLACK DAY, AND EVEN CHRISTMAS DAY--
AND CHRISTMAS NIGHT! OH, MY!
NO, IRENE! NO ECCHI THOUGHTS HERE! WE'RE KEEPING THIS MANGA FAMILY FRIENDLY!
AH! AS I WAS SAYING BEFORE BEING SO RUDELY INTERRUPTED, THERE ARE SEVERAL OTHER COUPLE HOLIDAYS IN KOREA BESIDES WHAT KENNY JUST MENTIONED.

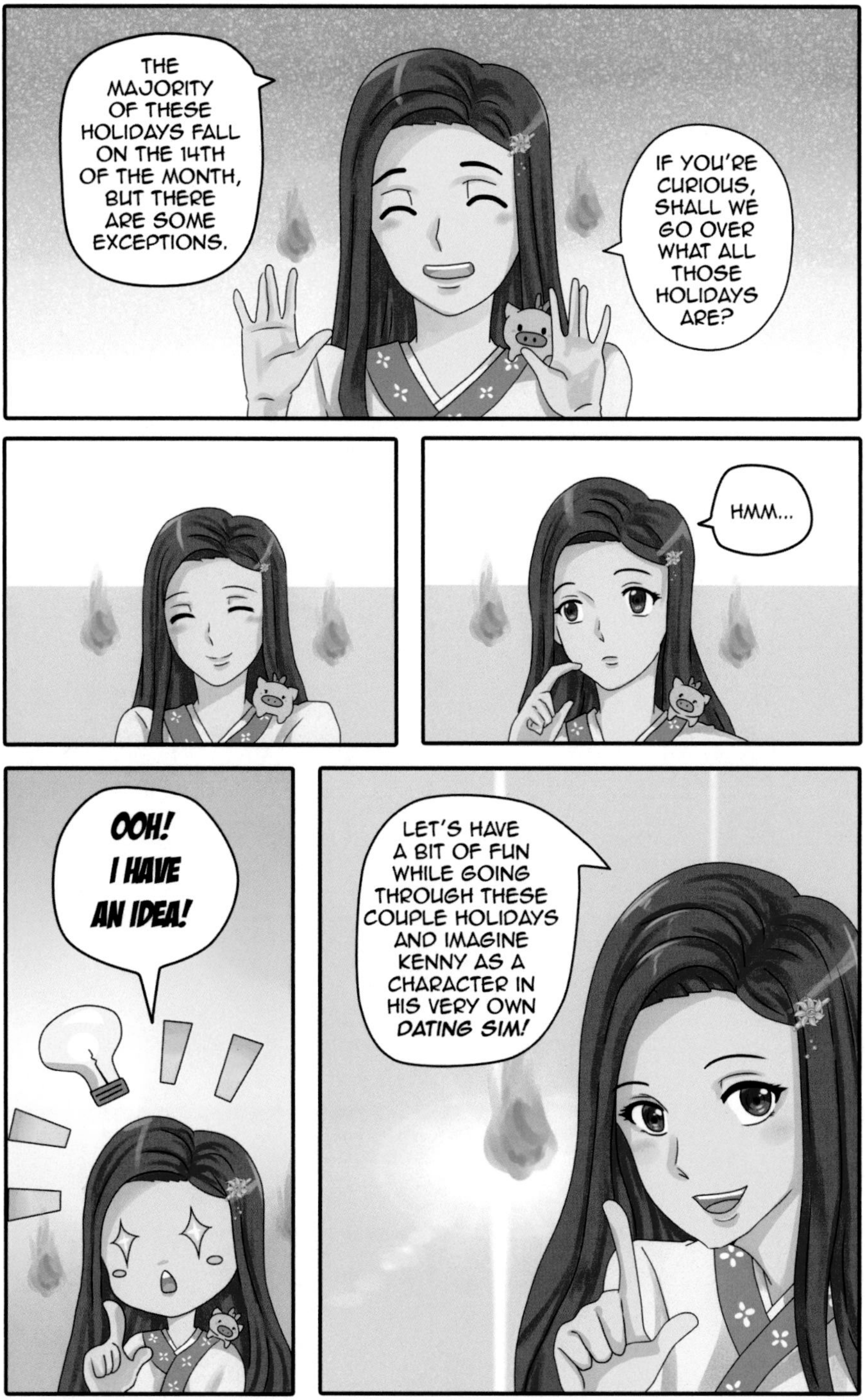
THE MAJORITY OF THESE HOLIDAYS FALL ON THE 14TH OF THE MONTH, BUT THERE ARE SOME EXCEPTIONS.
IF YOU'RE CURIOUS, SHALL WE GO OVER WHAT ALL THOSE HOLIDAYS ARE?
HMM...
OOH! I HAVE AN IDEA!
LET'S HAVE A BIT OF FUN WHILE GOING THROUGH THESE COUPLE HOLIDAYS AND IMAGINE KENNY AS A CHARACTER IN HIS VERY OWN DATING SIM!

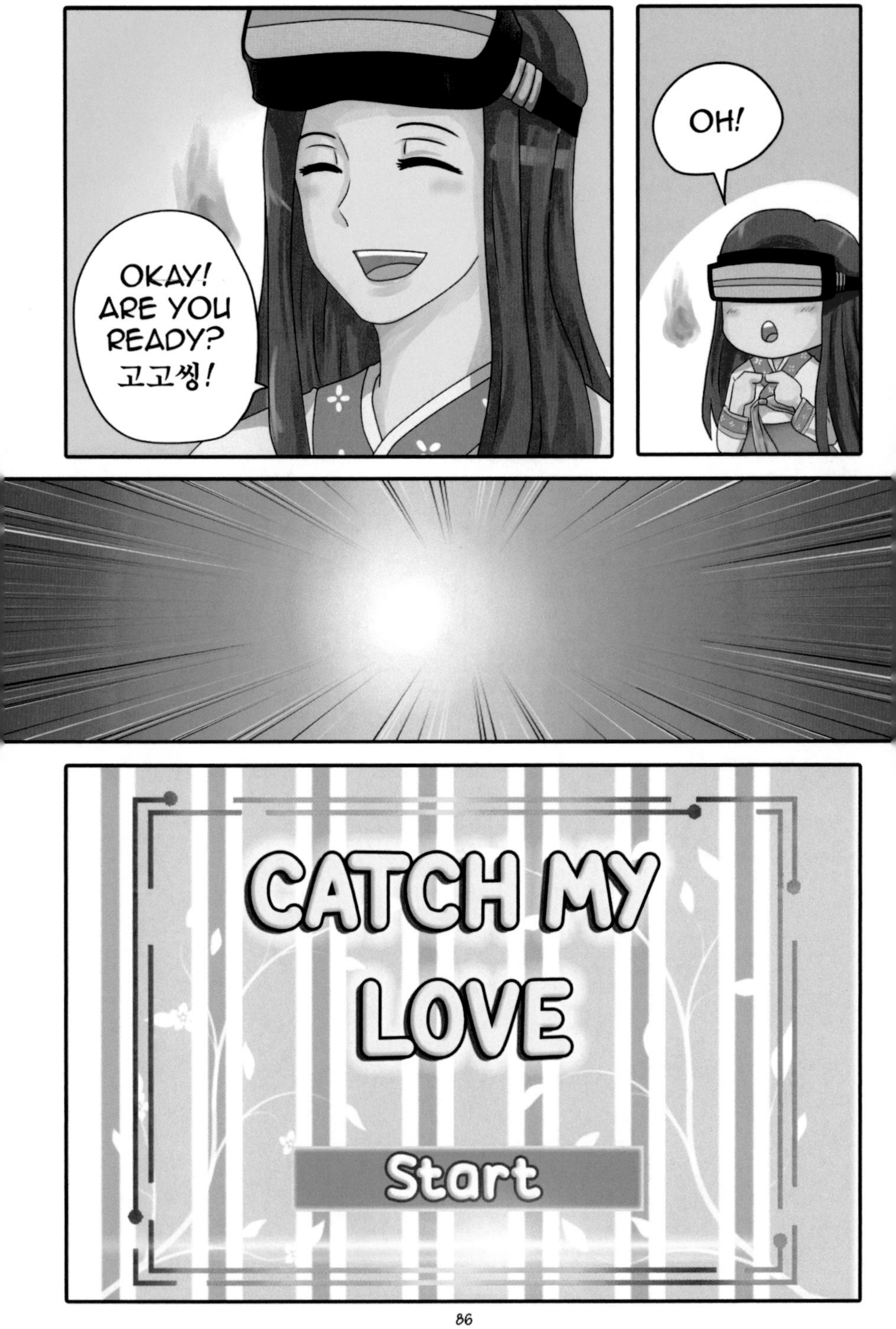
OKAY! ARE YOU READY? 고고씽!
OH!
CATCH MY LOVE
Start

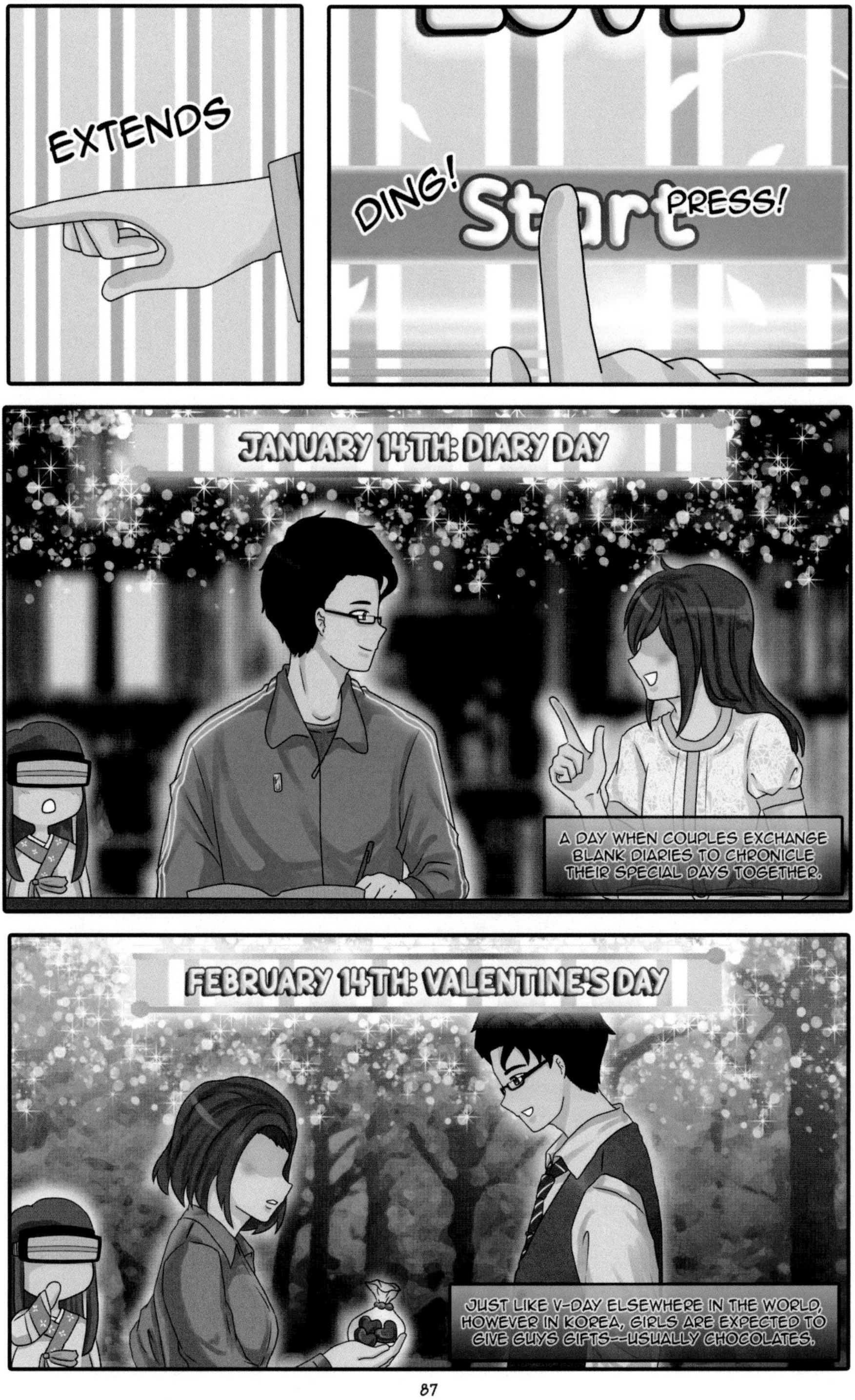
EXTENDS
DING!
Start
PRESS!
JANUARY 14TH: DIARY DAY
A DAY WHEN COUPLES EXCHANGE BLANK DIARIES TO CHRONICLE THEIR SPECIAL DAYS TOGETHER.
FEBRUARY 14TH: VALENTINE'S DAY
JUST LIKE V-DAY ELSEWHERE IN THE WORLD, HOWEVER IN KOREA, GIRLS ARE EXPECTED TO GIVE GUYS GIFTS--USUALLY CHOCOLATES.

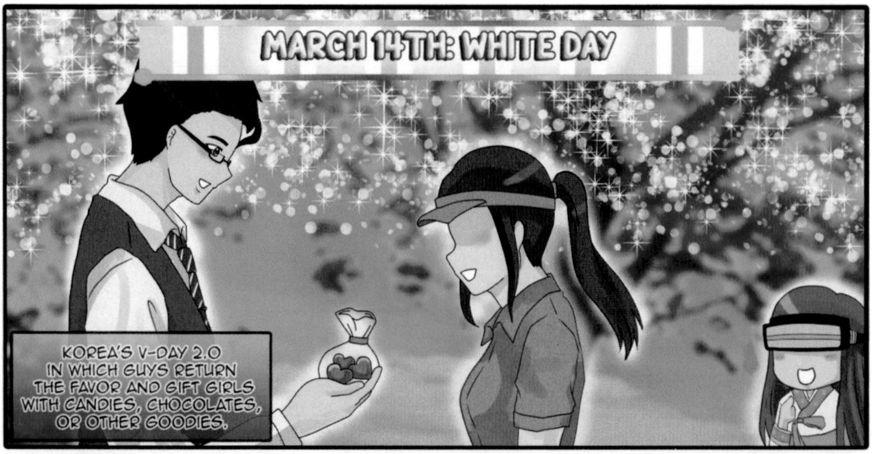
MARCH 14TH: WHITE DAY
KOREA'S V-DAY 2.0 IN WHICH GUYS RETURN THE FAVOR AND GIFT GIRLS WITH CANDIES, CHOCOLATES, OR OTHER GOODIES.

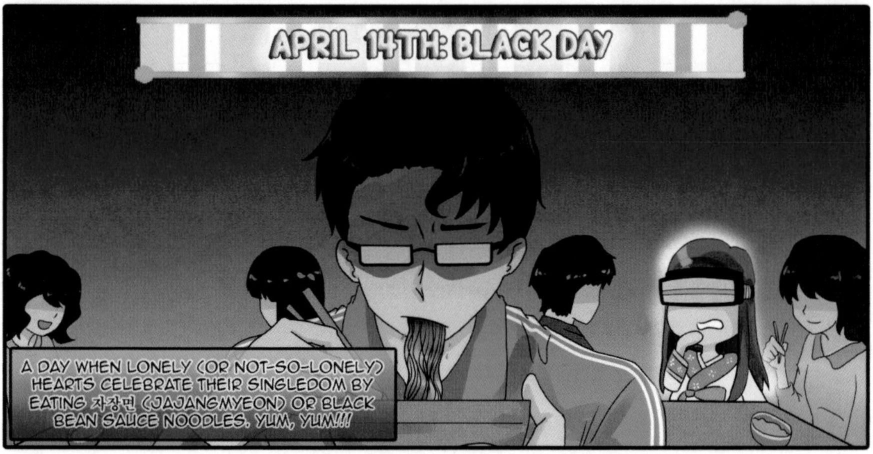
APRIL 14TH: BLACK DAY
A DAY WHEN LONELY (OR NOT-SO-LONELY) HEARTS CELEBRATE THEIR SINGLEDOM BY EATING 자장면 (JAJANGMYEON) OR BLACK BEAN SAUCE NOODLES. YUM, YUM!!!

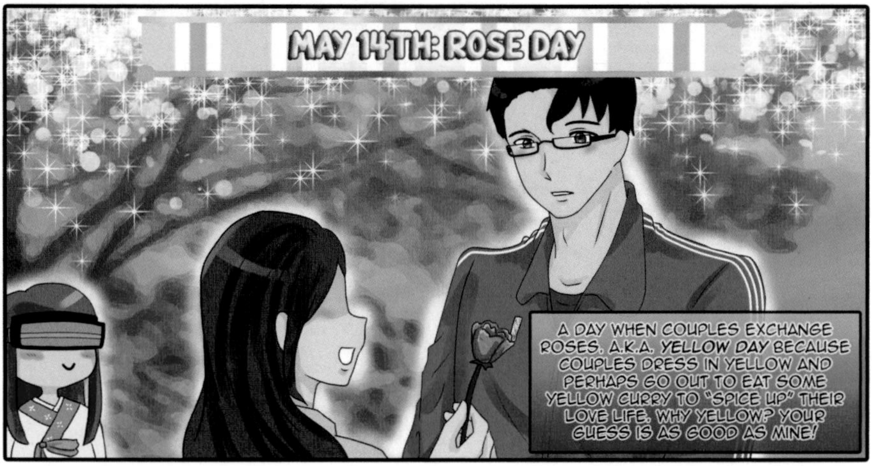
MAY 14TH: ROSE DAY
A DAY WHEN COUPLES EXCHANGE ROSES. A.K.A. YELLOW DAY BECAUSE COUPLES DRESS IN YELLOW AND PERHAPS GO OUT TO EAT SOME YELLOW CURRY TO "SPICE UP" THEIR LOVE LIFE. WHY YELLOW? YOUR GUESS IS AS GOOD AS MINE!

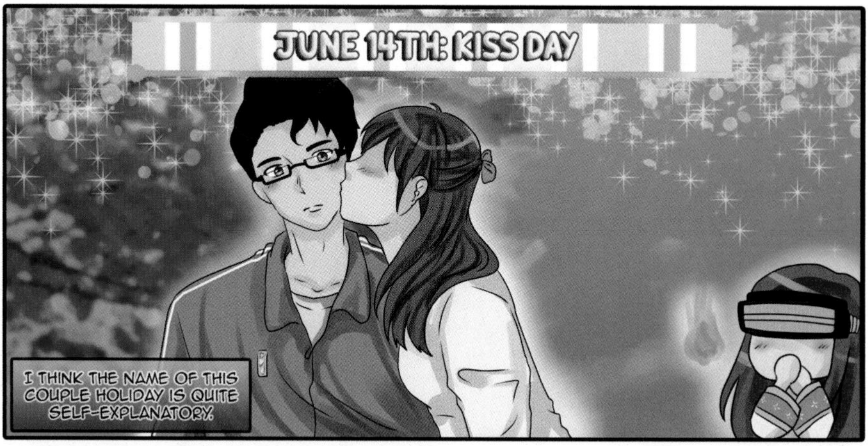
JUNE 14TH: KISS DAY
I THINK THE NAME OF THIS COUPLE HOLIDAY IS QUITE SELF-EXPLANATORY.

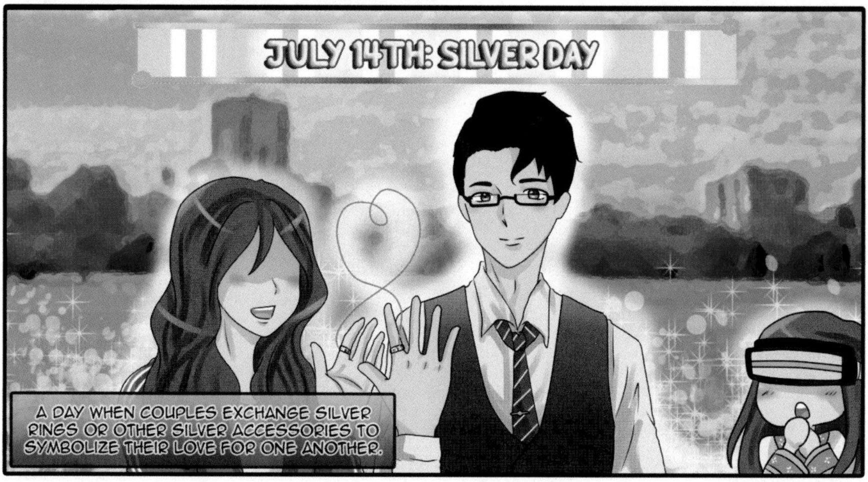
JULY 14TH: SILVER DAY
A DAY WHEN COUPLES EXCHANGE SILVER RINGS OR OTHER SILVER ACCESSORIES TO SYMBOLIZE THEIR LOVE FOR ONE ANOTHER.

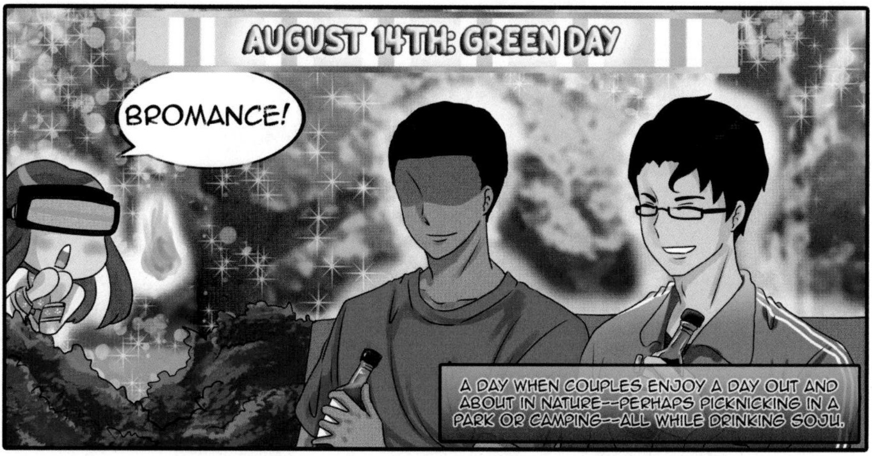
AUGUST 14TH: GREEN DAY
BROMANCE!
A DAY WHEN COUPLES ENJOY A DAY OUT AND ABOUT IN NATURE--PERHAPS PICKNICKING IN A PARK OR CAMPING--ALL WHILE DRINKING SOJU.

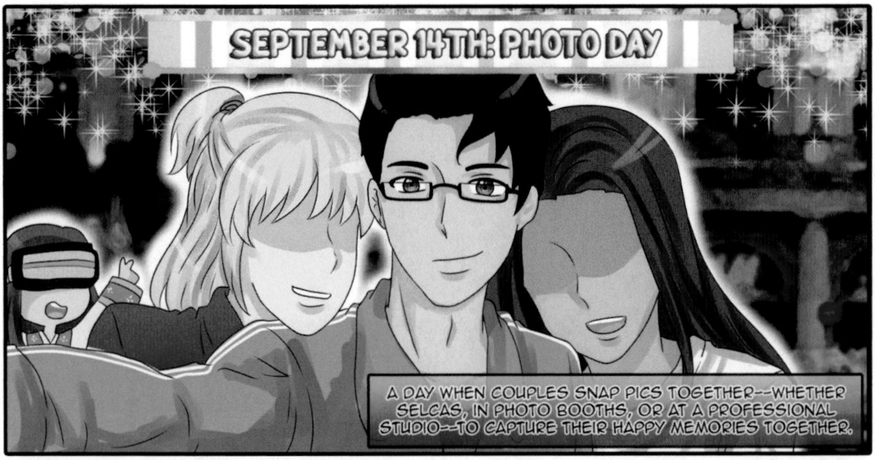
SEPTEMBER 14TH: PHOTO DAY
A DAY WHEN COUPLES SNAP PICS TOGETHER--WHETHER SELCAS, IN PHOTO BOOTHS, OR AT A PROFESSIONAL STUDIO--TO CAPTURE THEIR HAPPY MEMORIES TOGETHER.

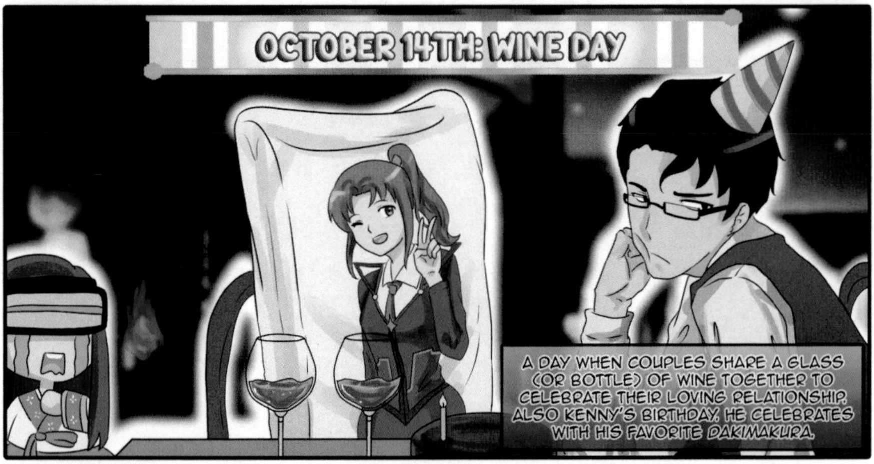
OCTOBER 14TH: WINE DAY
A DAY WHEN COUPLES SHARE A GLASS (OR BOTTLE) OF WINE TOGETHER TO CELEBRATE THEIR LOVING RELATIONSHIP. ALSO KENNY'S BIRTHDAY. HE CELEBRATES WITH HIS FAVORITE *DAKIMAKURA*.

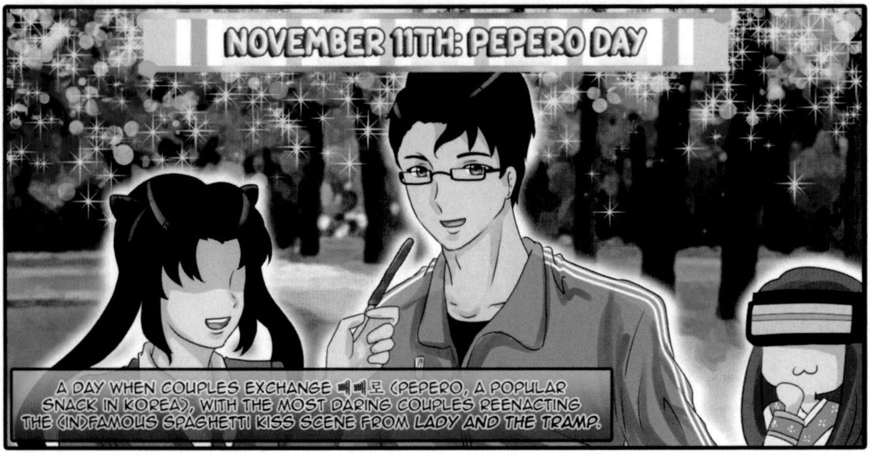
NOVEMBER 11TH: PEPERO DAY
A DAY WHEN COUPLES EXCHANGE 빼빼로 (PEPERO, A POPULAR SNACK IN KOREA), WITH THE MOST DARING COUPLES REENACTING THE (IN)FAMOUS SPAGHETTI KISS SCENE FROM *LADY AND THE TRAMP*.

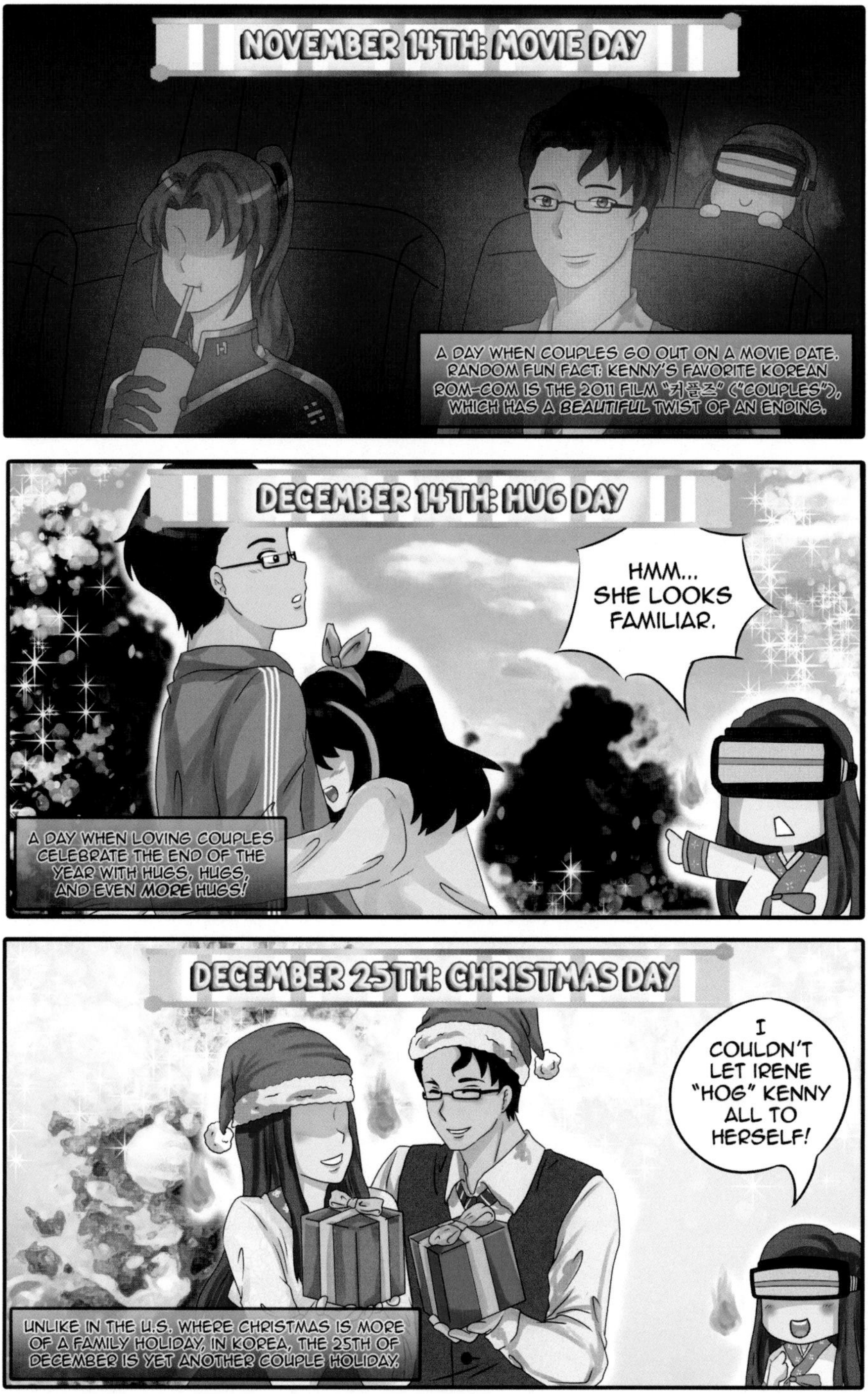
NOVEMBER 14TH: MOVIE DAY
A DAY WHEN COUPLES GO OUT ON A MOVIE DATE. RANDOM FUN FACT: KENNY'S FAVORITE KOREAN ROM-COM IS THE 2011 FILM "커플즈" ("COUPLES"), WHICH HAS A *BEAUTIFUL* TWIST OF AN ENDING.
DECEMBER 14TH: HUG DAY
HMM... SHE LOOKS FAMILIAR.
A DAY WHEN LOVING COUPLES CELEBRATE THE END OF THE YEAR WITH HUGS, HUGS, AND EVEN *MORE* HUGS!
DECEMBER 25TH: CHRISTMAS DAY
I COULDN'T LET IRENE "HOG" KENNY ALL TO HERSELF!
UNLIKE IN THE U.S. WHERE CHRISTMAS IS MORE OF A FAMILY HOLIDAY, IN KOREA, THE 25TH OF DECEMBER IS YET ANOTHER COUPLE HOLIDAY.

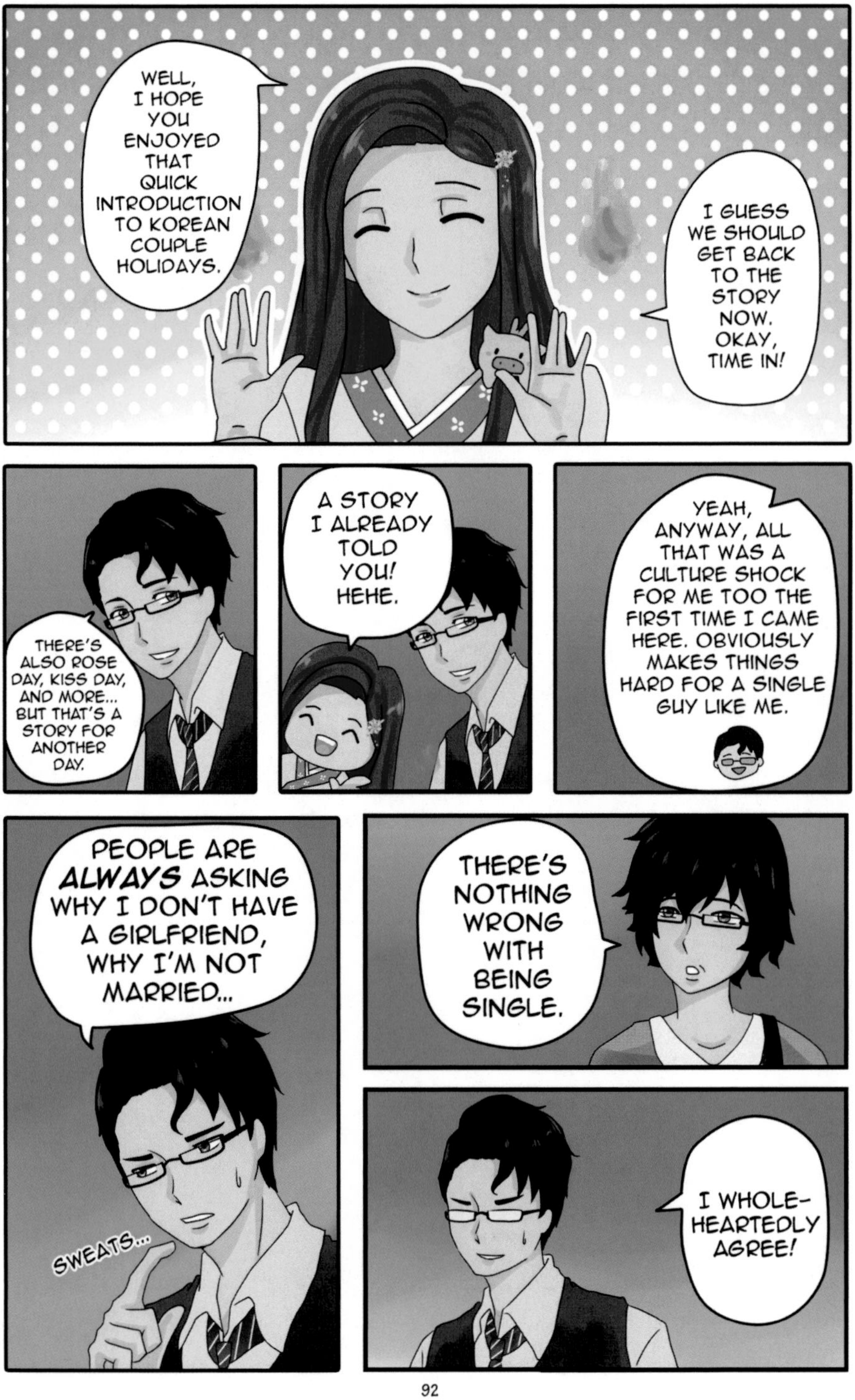
WELL, I HOPE YOU ENJOYED THAT QUICK INTRODUCTION TO KOREAN COUPLE HOLIDAYS.
I GUESS WE SHOULD GET BACK TO THE STORY NOW. OKAY, TIME IN!
THERE'S ALSO ROSE DAY, KISS DAY, AND MORE... BUT THAT'S A STORY FOR ANOTHER DAY.
A STORY I ALREADY TOLD YOU! HEHE.
YEAH, ANYWAY, ALL THAT WAS A CULTURE SHOCK FOR ME TOO THE FIRST TIME I CAME HERE. OBVIOUSLY MAKES THINGS HARD FOR A SINGLE GUY LIKE ME.
PEOPLE ARE ALWAYS ASKING WHY I DON'T HAVE A GIRLFRIEND, WHY I'M NOT MARRIED...
SWEATS...
THERE'S NOTHING WRONG WITH BEING SINGLE.
I WHOLE-HEARTEDLY AGREE!

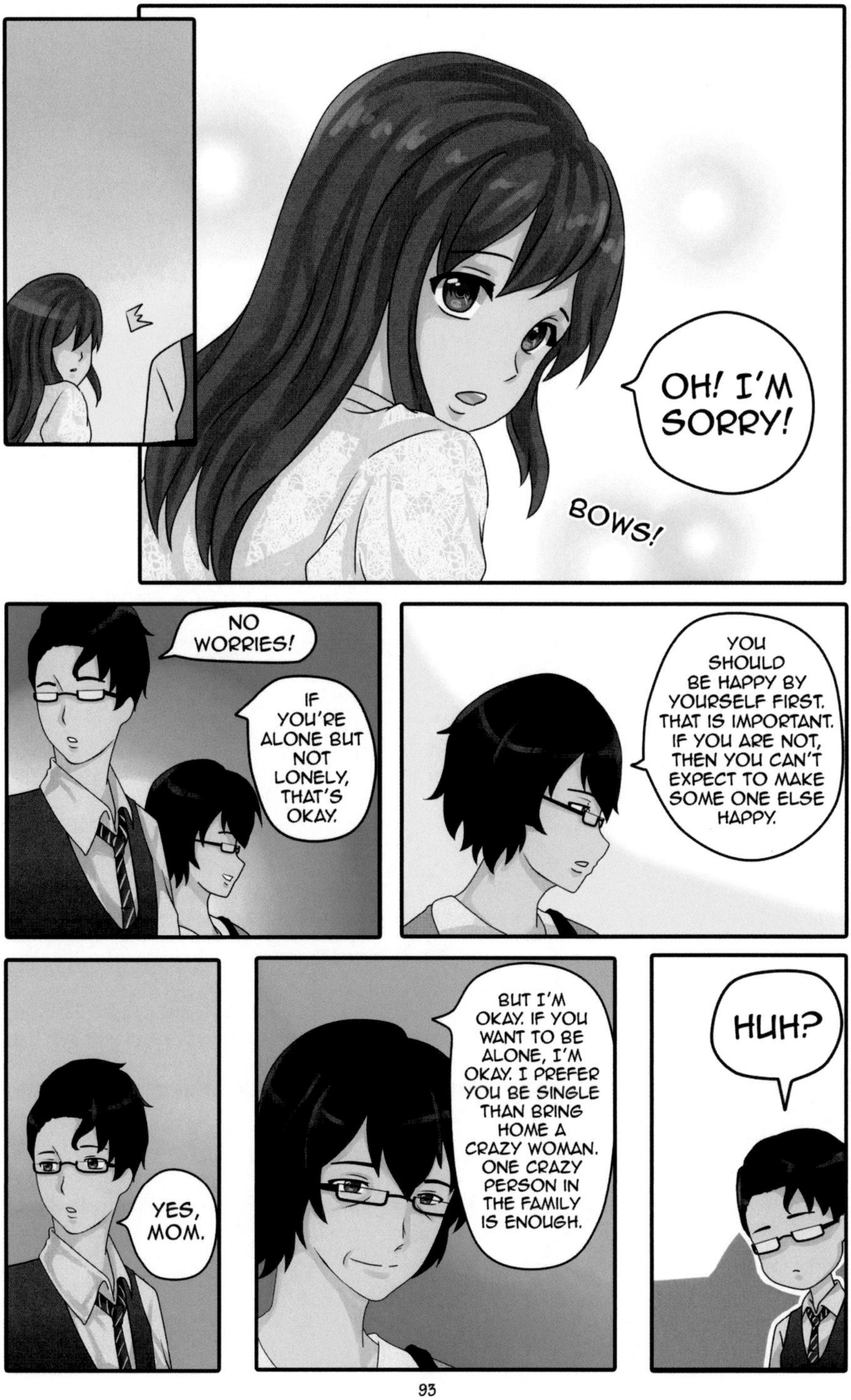

OH! I'M SORRY!
BOWS!
NO WORRIES!
IF YOU'RE ALONE BUT NOT LONELY, THAT'S OKAY.
YOU SHOULD BE HAPPY BY YOURSELF FIRST. THAT IS IMPORTANT. IF YOU ARE NOT, THEN YOU CAN'T EXPECT TO MAKE SOME ONE ELSE HAPPY.
YES, MOM.
BUT I'M OKAY. IF YOU WANT TO BE ALONE, I'M OKAY. I PREFER YOU BE SINGLE THAN BRING HOME A CRAZY WOMAN. ONE CRAZY PERSON IN THE FAMILY IS ENOUGH.
HUH?

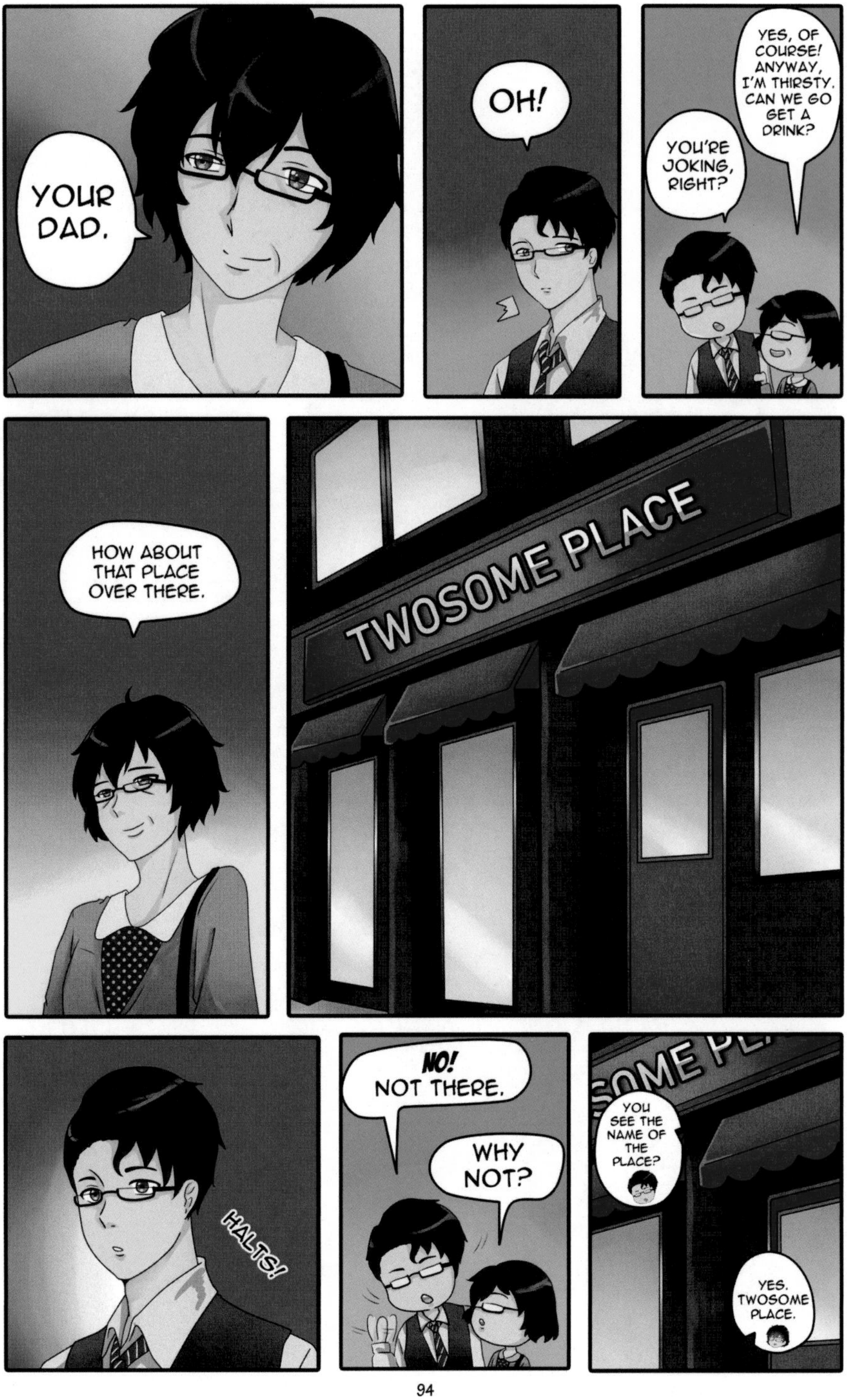
YOUR DAD.
OH!
YOU'RE JOKING, RIGHT?
YES, OF COURSE! ANYWAY, I'M THIRSTY. CAN WE GO GET A DRINK?
HOW ABOUT THAT PLACE OVER THERE.
TWOSOME PLACE
HALTS!
NO! NOT THERE.
WHY NOT?
YOU SEE THE NAME OF THE PLACE?
YES. TWOSOME PLACE.

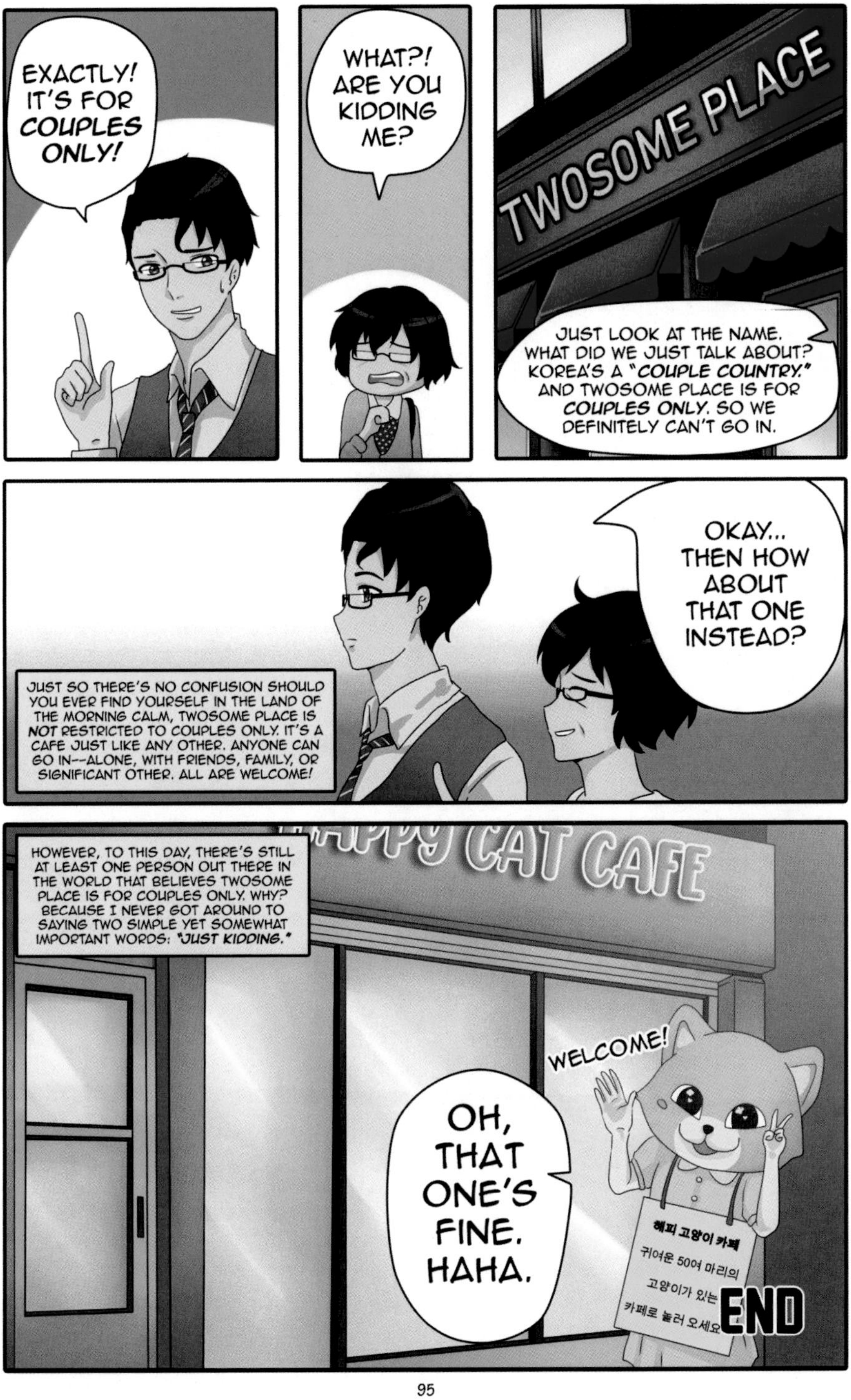
EXACTLY! IT'S FOR COUPLES ONLY!
WHAT?! ARE YOU KIDDING ME?
TWOSOME PLACE
JUST LOOK AT THE NAME. WHAT DID WE JUST TALK ABOUT? KOREA'S A "COUPLE COUNTRY." AND TWOSOME PLACE IS FOR COUPLES ONLY. SO WE DEFINITELY CAN'T GO IN.
OKAY... THEN HOW ABOUT THAT ONE INSTEAD?
JUST SO THERE'S NO CONFUSION SHOULD YOU EVER FIND YOURSELF IN THE LAND OF THE MORNING CALM, TWOSOME PLACE IS NOT RESTRICTED TO COUPLES ONLY. IT'S A CAFE JUST LIKE ANY OTHER. ANYONE CAN GO IN--ALONE, WITH FRIENDS, FAMILY, OR SIGNIFICANT OTHER. ALL ARE WELCOME!
HOWEVER, TO THIS DAY, THERE'S STILL AT LEAST ONE PERSON OUT THERE IN THE WORLD THAT BELIEVES TWOSOME PLACE IS FOR COUPLES ONLY. WHY? BECAUSE I NEVER GOT AROUND TO SAYING TWO SIMPLE YET SOMEWHAT IMPORTANT WORDS: "JUST KIDDING."
CAT CAFE
WELCOME!
OH, THAT ONE'S FINE. HAHA.
해피 고양이 카페
귀여운 50여 마리의
고양이가 있는
카페로 놀러 오세요
END

Memory Lane

FROM THE ARCHIVES OF U.F.O. CATCHER KEN

Memory Lane

FROM THE ARCHIVES OF U.F.O. CATCHER KEN

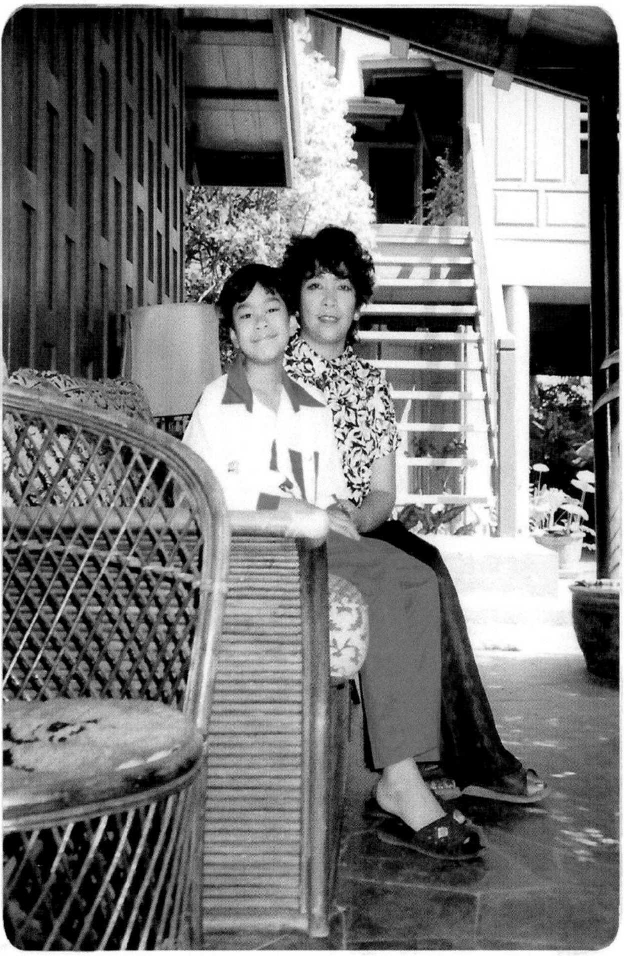

Life Lessons from a UFO Catcher®

An Autobiographical Manga

Story by Kenny Loui, Ph.D.

Art by Yamawe

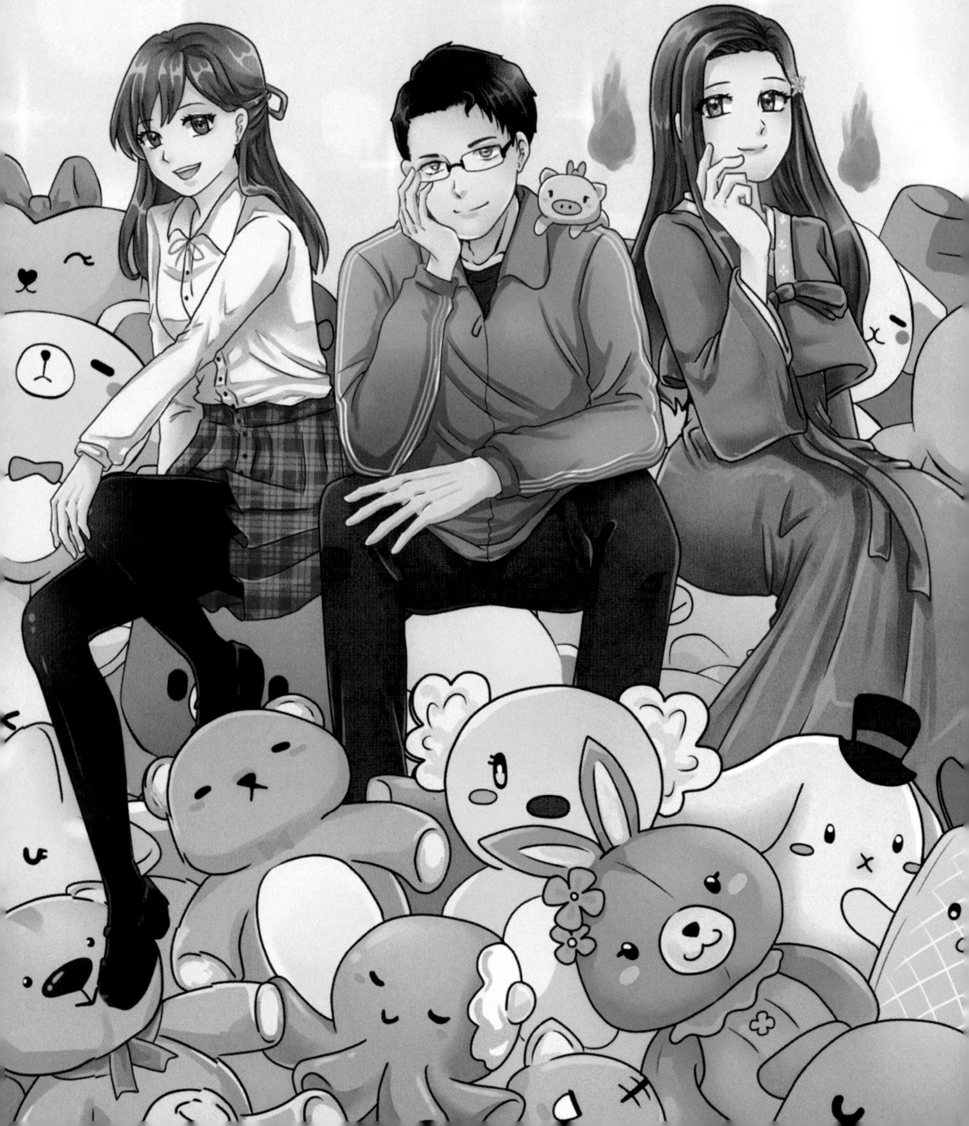

Kenny's UFO-catching adventures continue. But he now has an entourage—his twin sisters, Jinny and Sammy! Besides helping (and competing with) Kenny to liberate cute plushies trapped in arcade claw machines, Jinny and Sammy also attempt to rescue Kenny from his life of singledom by getting him out of the arcade and into the world of dating, love and romance!

Will Kenny find his true love or be left picking up the pieces of his broken heart? Find out in Season 2 of *Life Lessons from a UFO Catcher*!

WEBTOON CANVAS

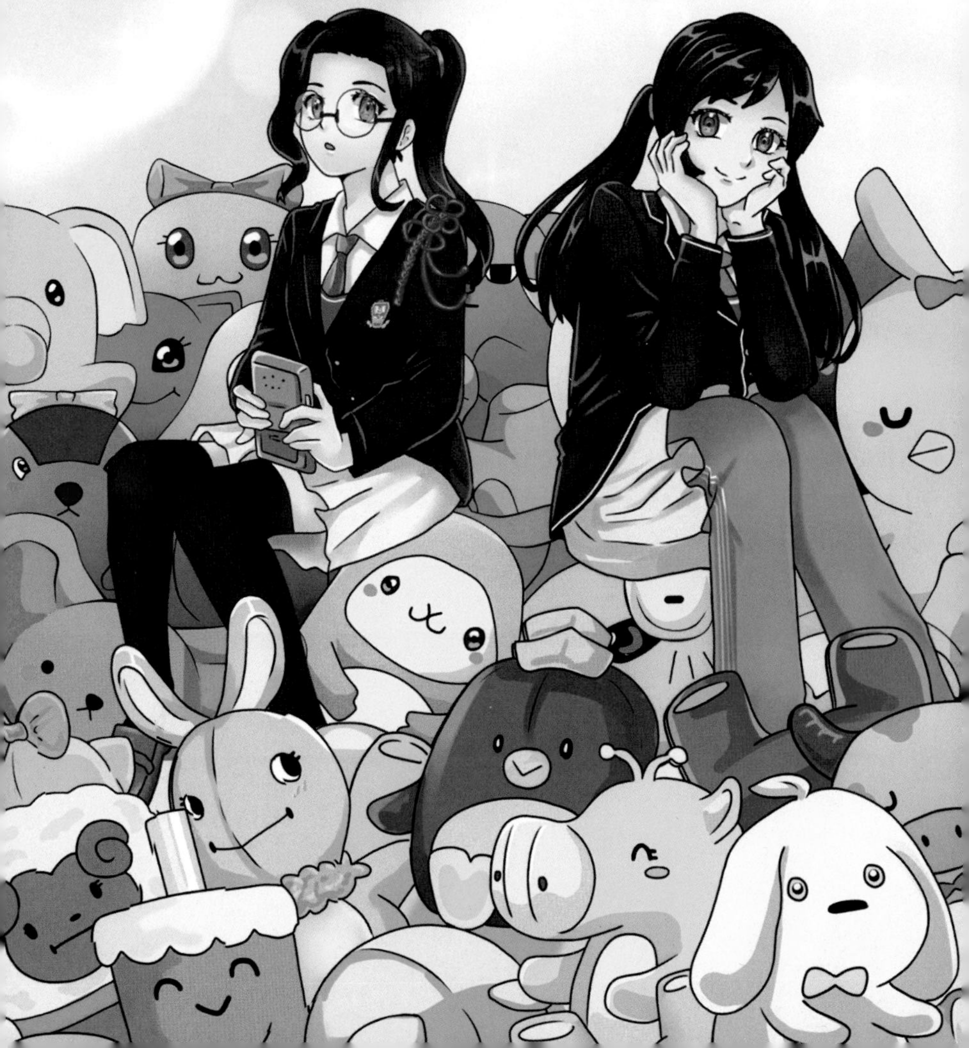

CREATORS

KENNY LOUI is a doctor (of philosophy), college professor, Civil Air Patrol officer, lifelong otaku, and professional third wheel. His hobbies include reading, writing, stargazing, and liberating cute and cuddly plushies trapped inside arcade crane games. He has been "UFO catching" since 2007 and has a rescue count of over 700 plush dolls, figures, and random thingamabobs.

AUTHOR

YAMAWE is a self-taught artist from the Philippines whose style draws inspiration from Japanese anime and manga. She holds a Bachelor of Information Technology and has been working as a freelance digital artist since 2014.

ARTIST

Made in the USA
Monee, IL
02 September 2023

42018198R00062